AF480968

BREAKING FREE

Healing from abuse and trauma

BRITTNEY GUARY

Breaking Free - Healing from abuse and trauma

By Brittney Guary

HE HEALS THE BROKENHEARTED AND BINDS UP
THEIR WOUNDS

Psalm 147:3

Table of Contents

Introduction

I always struggled trying to find my purpose in life and it wasn't until I was 33 years old that the light bulb turned on and everything made sense. Of course, we go through seasons in our lives where things may be one way for months or years before any change happens, but each season plays a critical part in our entire life purpose.

Through all the seasons, changes, challenges, difficulties, highs and lows that I've been through, they all helped me to figure out my purpose and write this book you're holding in your hands now.

Maybe you're like me and didn't have anyone teaching you your true identity; the woman God has created you to be and why He created you. No one taught you to whom you belong and with that, you don't know your true rights and what belongs to you. See, if you don't know to whom you belong, you won't know who you are. And if you don't know who you are you don't know what you're capable of. If you don't know what you're capable of, then you get tossed in the storms of life feeling defeated with every doctor's diagnosis; feeling alone in a sanctuary full of people, and always feeling you have to fight but you're just too weak to do so.

It's a vicious cycle. And then come relationships we chase to make things better, but in reality, they make them worse. We seek friendships to feel belongingness. Facebook groups and mommy dates to help us feel like we are a part of something important. And then we get into romantic relationships with Bozo trying to convince ourselves he's Boaz. We start acting like we enjoy everything he does in fear of rejection. Of course, at first, it's fun to try new things but over the months or for some of us even years later; we wake up and realize we've been compromising ourselves, getting more and more disconnected from the person God called us to be.

And Sis I'm speaking from a lifetime of experience the things I wish someone would have told me sooner, and I would have listened to. For the record, this book isn't to bash men or to say *all men are bad*. Because they aren't. I know many respectable men, outstanding fathers and father figures, romantic honest hard-working, and God-fearing young men and husbands. Protective brothers and phenomenal uncles.

I can hear y'all now asking *but where are they?* They are all around us Girl, hidden gems in plain sight just like you are. You just have to find your true self and you will start to see those hidden gems more clearly. The same goes for your business, your finances, your ability to create wealth, your family, your ministry and your friendships.

This is why I'm called to help other abused women know their true identity and heal so we can all come out of the muck and gunk; rise from our ashes, step into our calling, forgive, and walk in the victory that is intended for us! Then once we understand and fully know who we are, the fun part begins. The fight. And not just any fight. But the strategic, stealthy victorious fight.

We already know that God goes with us, before us, and gives us victory over our enemies. So all we have to do is put on our armor, listen carefully to His marching orders, and say, "Yes Lord send me." He does the rest.

This fight will get ugly and hard, and you may feel weary more than once; but don't give up because this next part is the most important. It's the heart of the battlefield. The longest part of the battle. It's the fight with yourself. You can fight the world and have some victory, but until you fight yourself and take out the thoughts that are killing you; you won't make it that far.

So crack your neck and knuckles, grab your sword, let out a victory cry and take your imposter self down. I'll get more into this imposter self later, but real quick, your imposter self is the version of you that is a lie. It's made up of all the lies you've been told and think about yourself.

I'm not worthy.
I'll always be alone.
I'm a horrible mother.
I'm a hypocrite.
I'm worthless.
I'll always be broke.
I can't create anything good.
I have no real purpose.
No one will actually love me and my kids.
My life is so messed up because of all my past sins.

You get it. Spoiler alert, all those things are lies! So that is the imposter self that we will be fighting against to reclaim our true identity, our purpose, our calling and our victory. And don't worry, it takes time, but you *can* do it!!! And I'm here to help you with this book. Once you take your imposter self out, the rest is like walking downhill. Still fighting, still a battle, but it's a whole lot easier than fighting uphill.

The enemy won't like it. Your boss won't like it; your family and friends may not even like it. It will make them uncomfortable that you're standing up for yourself. It will make them irritated that they can't control you. It will make them furious that the abuse no longer has an effect on you. Your narcissistic ex will be wrapped in a whirlwind of his own chaos, because he won't believe or understand how you made it out alive; and why his traps and lies are no longer entangling you. Your abuser will not only *feel* defeat, but will actually be defeated.

Stand strong, be courageous, be brave and don't cave in. When we have our family, friends, clients, business partners and the world against us, it can feel draining and at times alone. But you're not alone and I'm not leaving you unaware what to do next. Later chapters will help you live in your promised land.

I don't know about you but I'm excited now! As I write this I can already see the glory of God coming down exactly where you are, as you start wondering if this is even possible for someone like yourself. Someone who's been divorced, sexually abused, kidnapped, forced into marriage. You've lost your children, some to death or the court system and some have run away. You've been told over and over you're not good enough and no one will love you. Or that no one does love you, *(oh, but someone does)*. I promise you that.

You are loved by God; even now, and always will be loved. You get to accept or deny His love, but it's there either way. Not only does God love you through it all, there are honest people in this world who truly love you as well. *Me being one of them!* I'm not writing this book for my own personal gain, whatever that may be. I'm writing this book for you.

It's for the single mother of four who is divorced because of child abuse and has limited income; who fights every day not only to keep her children safe and have a roof over their heads. But more importantly she fights to help her children know they are loved and worthy and help them fight the lies that creep into their minds, ruining their hearts. And then finding time to do it for herself.

I write this book for heartbroken, depressed women who feel worthless and alone; afraid and beaten, forgotten and tormented by the voices of others and their own thoughts. Who sees no way out. For whom the death and burial of her own child buried her along with her baby's body. The woman who committed murder late one night because she was tired of all his abuse to her and her children. That shame and guilt and wishing you could just erase those last couple of seconds, but it's too late now. Let me tell you, it's not too late for you!

I write this for the woman who has been abandoned by all she knows, her family and friends, or so she thought. The woman whose very own church not only turned its back on you, and also got others to turn their backs on you as well. This book is dedicated to you because I know you all too well. I am that woman, too. But with everything I've gone through and everything I've faced; I will never let the past define who I am. And it stops for you too! Now! In Jesus' name.

If you're ready to become free, live in your promised land, meet your real self, fall in love with the One who created you and to whom you belong and claim your victory. If you're ready to accept your royal priesthood, accept the call on your life and walk in your anointing, destroy the lies you believe, and heal from the inside out; then you picked the right book.

Keep reading to the end. Share it with someone you know. And I want to hear all the testimonies of where you were when you started reading and where you are once you've finished this book.

You will find Bible scriptures. You will find *my* true story from an abusive marriage that ended in divorce, child services, homelessness, detectives, lawyers, and more court dates than I can count. You will also find declarations, prayers, and action steps to help you through your journey; so that **you can break free and heal.**

"I HAVE CALLED YOU BY NAME, YOU ARE MINE"

I was just trying to help. A family had graciously let me and my kids stay at their place in hiding for a short time while I figured out other living arrangements. I had to save every penny and I thought the investigation would move quickly, so I'd be back home shortly. I wanted to contribute however I could though.

So cleaning was the best way I knew how. I washed a sink full of dishes as if they were my own and set the last dish on the counter to dry. I cleaned out the sink and then it all happened in slow motion yet so fast I couldn't save it. The glass dish slid off the counter and hit the ground. In an instant it shattered into a million pieces, becoming completely unrecognizable all over the kitchen floor.

I could *hear* my heart stop beating, and after what felt like eternity, I finally gasped for breath. I grabbed for a remote to rewind time but there was no such thing. I desperately just wanted to rewind time for a second. I wanted this moment to not have happened. Like the second you hear the doctor say "I'm sorry, we did all we could." You just want to hold everything up and stop time itself from moving forward. But time keeps going with or without you. I lost all senses except my sight in that moment. I was huge in my twin pregnancy and just dropped to the ground and wept with not a single tear, as if I'd already cried them all out in the years leading to this life shattering moment.

As I tried to gather some of the pieces thinking I could somehow fix it; somehow, others had already been cleaning it up and getting the kids and dogs out the way. It was as if I were in a war movie after a bomb went off. Everything moving in slow motion and all you can hear is ringing in your ears, but my body was on autopilot trying to clean glass with my bare hands. It took a while before I caught up to reality. Pieces of glass shot all the way down the hall to the front door and over into the dining room area.

That was the moment I could visually see my life. All shattered in a million unrecognizable pieces that could only be thrown away. Too dangerous for others to be around. Too painful to handle myself. So far gone I'd never get it back. There was nothing I could have done and I'm still not sure how exactly it fell. I cleaned out the whole sink before it even hit the ground. Just like my life and my marriage, it shattered in a moment. I'll never forget that feeling and then the guilt that followed immediately after.

What this family must have thought of me. I was sure they wanted us out of their house even sooner now. They knew I'd offer to pay and I would buy a new one but they also knew the very little bit of money I had I was going to need. After all, we essentially were homeless. I felt like a worthless person and an undeserving mother.

How could I have married a man like this? Had I not, no one would have got abused, none of this would have happened.

Although the glass shattering was one hundred percent true and my feelings and thoughts were one hundred percent true; at that moment, I didn't know what I know now. I didn't know that my life wasn't over. That family didn't hate me for breaking the glass. They didn't even blame me or think twice. They cleaned it up and ordered a new one the same night.

When the new plate came, it was beautiful with no cracks, no missing pieces, no scratches. Just brand spanking new. I was afraid to touch it. I was afraid I'd break that one too. I was in shock and disbelief and almost envious of this new plate. It shatters, gets thrown away and then boom a couple of days later here it is all together and whole; brand new as if nothing happened to it. I know it was two different plates physically, but it was the same plate. I was still the shattered plate looking at the new, whole, unblemished plate, not realizing I was looking at myself through the eyes of my Maker.

When I first came to know the Lord, I heard about this woman who, by law at the time, was supposed to be murdered for committing adultery. Not only did she commit adultery, but she was caught in the very act; so there was no escaping this one. To be very honest I felt just like this woman. I just knew I wasn't going to escape punishment for all I'd done in my past. This had to be my punishment after all, wasn't it? What made me and this woman so relatable though was that she seemed to be very *accepting* of her punishment and she lost her identity. The identity God gave her at the start of her creation.

Most of us would have put up a huge fight if we got taken in by authorities to be killed. This woman just lay there. Ready for whatever was going to happen. Ready for unbearable punishment. Ready for death. I know she had to have thought it was better than all she had to endure in life now. Right? Isn't that what we all think about ourselves? This physical pain is nothing compared to the hurt I have inside. I can endure the physical pain just as long as it's going to stop *all* the pain all together soon.

I've had tons and tons of these kinds of self-sabotaging thoughts.

"I deserve being homeless with no income, two kids plus pregnant with twins, going through a divorce, with an abusive narcissist at that. I knew I didn't want to go through with the marriage let alone start talking to him in the first place. I saw tons of red flags. But I still did it anyway. I had a choice and I still choose to follow through. This is what I get. I shouldn't even expect anything better of him because he showed me signs of his true self long before engagement. I had this one coming to me. This is what I get!"

I got wrapped in a whirlwind of lies, shame, and guilt that led me to just *accept* my punishment. And that wasn't my first time thinking like that unfortunately.

I honestly had worse thoughts when I lost my first son. I never got to meet him. Never got to hold him. It was a choice to give birth early for my own safety although, at the time, I didn't care about my own life. I just wanted my son to be okay and alive. It felt like the biggest scam of my life. I was told the third part of his skull was not forming properly and that he would die before he was born. The longer I stayed pregnant the worst the effects could have been on me and I could possibly have died or been extremely ill at the very least.

I knew nothing about pregnancy or how any of this worked. So much so, I didn't even know I was in an abortion clinic being "induced," so I was told by medical doctors, at a hospital hours from where I lived. I went into the hospital to give birth and to my surprise they injected a "tranquilizer to stop the baby's heart;" that's the last thing I remember the nurse saying before I woke up in a recovery hallway. I was lying on my stomach with blood on my gown that was up by my shoulders; and my son was gone just like that. When I asked to speak to the doctor, the nurse looked at my chart and said I'm wasn't allowed.

I left the hospital in Philadelphia childless, clueless and heartless. It started a downhill spiral of marijuana, cocaine, wine, liquor, beer, sex, stripping, suicidal acceptance and anything to take my thoughts to a different world. I was never as bad as I became after the death of my son. But I still blamed myself and believed, "this is what I get."

Much like this woman who was brought out in public against her will, lying completely exposed on the ground; just accepting and waiting to be killed. This is how we feel when our life comes crashing down on us.

You get a divorce, you lose a child too early, you lose your spouse to addiction. You kill a family by driving after drinking, you are trapped in an abusive relationship; you were forced to marry at a young age to an old man, or any forced marriage. Your dad raped you as a young teen and now you're pregnant. You're watching your child fight stage four cancer.

We all have our lows. Our breaking points. The point where we no longer *feel* completely defeated, but we truly believe we *are* defeated and empty. Where a million thoughts no longer run through our minds, but only *one*. A single thought.

One time.

And then blank.

"This is what I get"

" I was still the

shattered plate

looking at the new,

whole, unblemished

plate, not realizing I was

looking at myself

through the eyes of my

Maker. "

The fact that I could relate to her, feel her pain, and know her thoughts was what intrigued me. But what happened next was what became monumental for me. It was a shifting in not only my mind but my heart.

Jesus says in John 8 whoever has no sin to cast the first stone.

"...Jesus stooped down and started writing on the ground with his finger. When they persisted in questioning him, he stood up and said to them, 'The one without sin among you should be the first to throw a stone at her.' Then he stooped down again and continued writing on the ground."

First of all, can we just take note of how Jesus got down on the ground with this woman. The King of Kings got down on her level with her. With the adulterous woman who was to be killed for her actions. In modern days we don't think of adultery as something to be killed for. Nowadays, adultery is really only frowned upon if the pastor does it. For the sake of generations, it's like this woman is someone who walked into someone else's house and shot and killed the whole family. Then the police show up and take her into custody. Now she is before the judge and jury listening to the police demand that she be punished by the death sentence. She should be electrocuted or euthanized. And the judge comes down from his seat and sits next to her. Not angry, just peacefully and tells the whole courtroom that whoever has never lied in any capacity, not even a small white lie, ever in their entire life from the time they were born until now, can take her and kill her themselves.

Deep, right? Let's go deeper. John 8:8-11 everyone left and "*When Jesus stood up, he said to her, 'Woman, where are they? Has no one condemned you?' 'No one, Lord,' she answered. 'Neither do I condemn you,' said Jesus. 'Go, and from now on do not sin anymore.'*"

She acknowledges that this man is Lord right from the beginning! The very fact she calls him Lord proves she knows who this man is, the Messiah, the Judge, the only One who knows her and has the authority to punish her worse than the stoning would have done. She is showing her shame and guilt. She is accepting of the punishment she is owed here. She is repentant of her sins.

Now I know you're probably thinking this book was supposed to help you because you're the victim here. You've been abused and mistreated and damaged. But hang on because this part of the story is critical. Whatever sin or wrongs you've done in your past, do not excuse the hurt, pain and trauma that you endured, and they never will.

Yes, we all must acknowledge our sin and deal with it, but not allow the enemy to attack us here and make us feel like everything we went through was because we messed up. That's why you got beat and that's why you were raped. No. That was pure evil doing what it does. Stealing, killing and destroying. This is about knowing you are called and known by Christ no matter what you did or what you've been through! This intense peaceful moment He tells her that He doesn't condemn her. He lets her go. Why? Because He *knows* her. Her posture was one of repentance. The same way *He knows you*. And loves you deeply.

No matter what you've done or what's been done to you in your life, He still loves you. He wants you to spend eternity with Him and the Father. He wants to give you good gifts and blessings and favor in abundance and overflowing ten-fold. More than you can think or imagine. And I think it's safe to say as a woman we have no problem with imagining.

But the very first thing we must do is acknowledge He is Lord and then repent of our sins, move on, and heal.
 She saw herself as unclean and unworthy, ashamed, and unloved. But God sees her as chosen, and righteous, forgiven and loved, cherished, and anointed. God sees you for more than who you think you are. God sees you in the image He created you. "Let us make them in our image; after our likeness." He says. God already knew the plans for you before you were born. He knit you together in your mother's womb and anointed you. You have a plan and purpose that God created in you. You are fully known by Him.

You just have to learn who you are too. Once you begin to know who God is, you will have a better understanding of who you are. And the beautiful thing is, this works both ways. Keeping in mind that you were created in His image and likeness; you will be able to know who God is as you discover who you really are.

Although your life may be shattered now, there is hope. The abuse you've endured will always be a part of your life that you can't rewind or change, but one day you will be able to look at yourself through the eyes of Christ and see yourself the way He sees you. You will be whole, unblemished, and new because you are chosen and redeemed, and He calls you by name.

BREAKING FREE

I have placed these exercises throughout this book to help you walk through, overcome, and heal. Grab a journal and remember the adulterous woman. Think of all the feelings, thoughts, and emotions she must have felt at the time of being completely exposed before everyone.
She must have felt ashamed, traumatized, scared, hurt, unworthy, like a caged animal. I'm sure you can relate to these feelings as much as I can.

I hate to be the one to tell you this if you don't already know, but healing hurts. The only way to properly heal is to dig out the infection; but when we dig out the infection and the healing process begins everything else lines up beautifully. And that's when we can call ourselves healed. So I know this exercise is going to be painful for all of you. It was painful for me. But it couldn't be more important. And we can move on. This isn't to keep you stuck in pain, it's only to get to the core of it so we can remove it fully. When you take it out at the root or from the core, it can't come back.

So I want you to first think back and remember that final breaking point for you. That moment you felt at your absolute lowest. The time you felt like completely giving up. The time you felt the most ashamed and the most exposed. That time that your world came crashing down, and for some of us, it was the time we almost took our life. It may have been once or it may have been many times. But write down all the feelings, thoughts and emotions *you* had, and still may have, when you've come to that place of giving up. That exposed place of just accepting whatever happens. That place where you've lost your identity.

After you write your thoughts, emotions and feelings down, pray that God takes those lies that are rooted deep down inside your heart and fills your heart with His truth and love. Don't overthink the prayer. When you mean it with your heart, you don't need an elaborate prayer. It's a simply us praying, "Lord please take all the lies that I believe about myself, take all the pain and thoughts that are not Yours and exchange it for Your truth. Show me who I really am, in You." In Jesus' name Amen.

Now, across from the negative word, the lie that you wrote down, write the positive; the promises, the identity that God has given you. You may not know any. So I did provide an example list, which is 100% true. The characteristics on the right side are the things that God says about you, who you are, and how He feels about you. So use every single one of those words. And continue to add the things God is revealing to you. Whatever positive thoughts pop in your head about yourself, write those down. *I am strong, happy, resilient, patient, etc.* As you move through this book and your healing journey, come back and keep adding to this list.

Whatever is true, whatever is honorable, whatever is right, whatever is pure, whatever is lovely, whatever is commendable, if there is any excellence and anything worthy of praise, *think about these things.*

Ashamed	Confident
Unworthy	Worthy
Unloved	Loved
Betrayed	Wanted
Abandoned	Adopted
Rejected	Accepted
Insecure	Anointed
Condemned	Chosen
Lonely	Healed
Isolated	Wonderfully made
Hurt	I have purpose
Traumatized	Courageous
I'm Suffocating	I'm Free
Trapped	Forgiven
Paralyzed	Joyful
Numb	Wise

Make sure you say these things out loud too. Use your voice. It's powerful. You don't have to believe it yet but by using your voice and your words, you will break down the walls. The Lord uses our voices for victory. The walls of Jericho fell with a loud shout. David killed Goliath with a stone and sling shot right after he shouted out to Goliath across the valley that he came against him in the name of the Lord of Armies. Shout a war cry. Shout joyfully to the Lord. Job 8:21 He will yet fill your mouth with laughter and your lips with shouting. In Matthew 21:15 the children were shouting "Hosanna the Son of David." Shouts of joy. Even wisdom calls aloud as she raises her voice. Psalm 1:20. Revelations 19:1 says a loud voice of a great multitude in heaven, saying, "Hallelujah! Salvation and glory and power belong to our God.

Our voice is powerful. And there is life and death in the power of your tongue.

So proclaim your God given truths out loud every day. And let His word sink into your heart "I have called you by name. YOU ARE MINE!" Says the Lord.

2

UNMASKING ABUSE

For me one of the hardest things to accept was the fact that I was a victim of abuse in my marriage. For some reason I could accept it from my past relationships. I knew I got beat, cheated on, and manipulated in my other non married relationships. I knew I faced trauma from the death of my son and that whole experience scared me for life. But accepting the fact that I had been abused in my marriage was the hardest part for me. Marriage isn't supposed to be full of lies, cheating, lack of communication, bondage and anything that doesn't make you feel safe.

Abuse is an action that happens repeatedly and is the *misuse* of something for a *bad purpose*, to *injure* or *damage*. Of course while you're in the middle of abuse, things seem wrong to you but it's not fully clear yet that you are in fact being abused. But once you're out. it's like a cover is lifted from your eyes and things make much more sense. Some take longer to see it than others and that's okay as long as you're out and safe. Your safety is what matters most right away. The healing process comes later. And this is in no way shaming anyone who stays in abuse. Again, I escaped. And as happy as I was to have escaped, I realized and completely understood why women stay in abusive situations. It is easier. But your freedom is worth the fight. Your safety and your children's safety is worth the fight. Don't take the easier way. Get out.

You will never be fully healed until you accept the fact that you are a victim of abuse and acknowledge the trauma you went through. Not everything is abuse and not everything causes trauma, but you'd be surprised at the things that *are* in fact abuse. There are several categories of abuse and many forms of abuse under each category.

Most of us only think of physical abuse, hitting, throwing, punching, choking, etc. Or child abuse, there are many subcategories here from physical child abuse, sexual child abuse, emotional, neglect, mental, etc. Or we think of sexual abuse only being rape. Sexual abuse is also any unwanted sexual actions done to you by another. Babysitter, parent, relative, partner, a girl friend "being curious," co-worker or boss, even your husband. Sexual abuse is also forced prostitution. Someone making you have sex or do any sexual pleasure for another person or to pay your rent,

keep your job or "for your safety" as an abuser would say.
These things cause serious trauma.

But that's not all. Most of us face abuse and trauma from
things we would never think of as abuse until we're out of it
or have gone to counseling or read this book. I'll start with
the forms of abuse that I went through most recently in
marriage.

FINANCIAL ABUSE

Financial abuse was the most obvious for me although at
the time I didn't know financial abuse existed. I just knew
while it was happening to me, I hated it! Before I got
married I talked several times with my ex about my staying
home with the kids and working from home so I could
continue to homeschool them. He agreed. After we got
married he told me I needed to put my kids in public school
and go to work. Mind you I wasn't a crazy spender and
when I did want something or even needed something I
always thrifted or shopped around for the best deal. Very
much opposite of how he did things, but I love a deal and
being a single mom for years; it only makes sense to be
frugal. When we got married I also thought of our money
as *our* money. So of course I wanted to see security in the

bank with months of rent and bills stored; should something happen and a nice savings account for buying a home, *so I thought.*

When I was told I had to get a job outside of the home, I was devastated. And honestly it wasn't the job part, it was sending my kids to public school; when I knew I felt God calling me to homeschool them, and the fact that he was *telling* me what I had to do. I had no say other than which job I was going to take, as long as I was home to get the kids to school in the morning; and pick them up from school in the evening because he wasn't doing it. Then he would leave for extended weekends for these business conferences that he wouldn't do any work for, and leave me home with no money if I couldn't go because of my new work schedule. One time he sent me to one of these meetings without him and gave me a card that had no money on it. Then refused to send me money any other way. Talk about embarrassing, humiliating and pathetic. *My phone just gave me that word pathetic and it fit perfectly but I was going to say how unloved and uncared for it made me feel.*

Your *freedom* is worth the fight.

This is financial abuse. The very little bit of money I was making, I had to use it all before asking him for more. He was on my health insurance so I didn't get much of a pay check every week. He brought in thousands of dollars every single week. The kids had to be on another insurance and he was supposed to pay that. He would refuse and their insurance bill became higher and higher. He didn't even care. It sat on the counter and I reminded him every chance I got, until I finally got a hold of his bank card and just paid it all.

A whole year I saved what I could to go to Israel for a mission trip. I had a thousand dollars saved of my own money. He told me to take seven hundred dollars out to pay for a puppy that we didn't need at the time. He said he'd give me the money right back but he couldn't get to the bank in time. It made more sense to me to wait until after our trip to get a puppy but he insisted. Long story short, while in Israel, he still didn't give my money back and held off shopping until I decided to walk through Jerusalem alone so I could buy gifts with the three hundred I had left.

And that's just a very few examples. I had very limited control. There was no compromise and when I tried to plead my case calmly, then again in tears, and again in anger, and again numb; he ignored me each and every time. Every. Single. time. This is abuse.

CONTROL

Controlling you as if you were a child with no rights. Most children get more say than I did in my marriage, but not me or my children. Control is a form of abuse and it's traumatizing as well. Control usually is best seen with manipulation.

My ex would tell me I *need* to get a job and put the kids in public school so that *I* would enjoy the break from them. Mind you I never complained about homeschool. At times it's rough, but I knew this was our calling for my children and overall I enjoyed it way more than I ever had a bad day teaching them. Not to mention they loved it. But my ex and his mom hated the idea. Control also looks like his taking my daughter's Apple iPod Touch that she had for a couple of years prior to my even knowing him; and he hid it and refused to give it back with no reason. He just said "No."

Another battle I tried desperately to win, especially since she had to go to public school; she needed a way to communicate with me. At that time, she was in fourth grade in an area where we didn't know anyone, and all this was new to us again. She only did preschool and kindergarten before. So for me this new situation was scary and triggered a past traumatic experience.

In preschool I went to pick her up and they said she wasn't there the day my brother dropped her off. That preschool experience was terrifying to me. I was running through the school yelling her name, then running outside realizing she could be anywhere in this whole world, dead, alive, scared. Who knows? Come to find out my brother dropped her off at daycare that day and she was safe.

But you see how trauma affects other areas in your life. We will get into that more later too. If you notice you're not being heard and only told what to do, especially with life changing situations and no compromise, you're being controlled. If someone is trying to make you side with them on things you are against but they try to make it seem as if *you* really do want it for reasons that only satisfy them; then you're being manipulated.

I am a Christian and I believe in having a relationship with Jesus Christ. And I believe what the Bible tells us about praying and staying in constant communication with Him, and I love it. I've seen God move in my own life and others. I've seen miracles happen and prayers answered. I even had a little prayer book that I could keep track of prayers that were prayed and when they were answered. I personally struggled with fibromyalgia for years before coming to the Lord and I was completely healed and haven't had any fibromyalgia pains or problems since 2015. My prayers about our marriage took the longest. Honestly, I don't recall one of them being answered; until one night I prayed God's Will be done in our marriage because I was below low and I came to terms with just living like this until one of us died. I really thought God hated divorce more than our wellbeing. *That's for another chapter, possibly a whole other book.* But my ex knew I was like this and I guess because I had a better relationship with God than him and he knew God was *going* to step in, my ex worried. This is my assumption, because that's when he threw bombs, really at God, but directed to me. He led me to believe prayers don't work. So much so I ended up tearing apart my prayer closet. Ripped up all my written prayers and threw them out while feeling numb and sobbing all at the same time.

See, just like the serpent in the garden questioning Eve, I too started questioning if what he was saying could be true.

Yes, I had seen many other answered prayers, but my marriage was still falling apart more and more over time.

Maybe my prayers weren't working. But they did before. What changed? Is it because we became one and only one of us was clearly praying? If that's the case, I'd rather have Jesus than this marriage. But God wouldn't leave me like that. Right? Don't You hate divorce God? If I can't get through to Him and You won't get through to him am I supposed to leave You too? That doesn't seem like the God I've known. I've been faithful and He loves each one of us because of who we are not who we married. Is this my punishment for getting married? Is this payback for all the sin I asked forgiveness for? So you don't really wipe out all our sins and forgive us like it says in Your word? No, I'm thinking crazy. You forgave me. You love me. But why haven't You fixed our marriage? Why haven't our hearts turned? What am I doing wrong? Are You even listening right now? What's the point of praying anymore if you stopped listening. Maybe my prayers don't work. This is what I get. I'm sorry God, please forgive me, if You're really listening.

These were my real thoughts and prayers to God. And I'm sure I had more, but they all kept going back and forth like this. So I understand if you feel the same way about whatever it is you've been through or are going through. I promise you it's all lies from the enemy to make you question and doubt and turn away from God. That's what the enemy wants you to do; leave God on your own will. And all it takes is for him to whisper a question in your ear. This is why knowing who you are and your true identity like we touched on in the last chapter is so critical to your healing.

I disagreed with him. I told him he was wrong and God does answer prayers. But his words attacking us felt so real. So much so that when I would pray, I would not stop and give God a chance to talk to me; so I really felt like he wasn't listening. But really it was me that wasn't listening. Until I had no more words, no more thoughts, and I just lay there before him, exposed and accepting whatever happens, happens. It wasn't until that moment when I began to hear his gentle voice again.

Spoiler alert, **Prayers DO work.** Don't let anyone tell you otherwise. You may not get exactly what you prayed for, when you pray it, or the way you prayed for it. Some prayers take days, years, decades, or even generations to be answered. And of course they have to line up with God's will. You won't always know what His will is but if you stay in relationship with Him, He will guide your heart. Most people want a million dollars to give away and buy a home and pay off debt, but God doesn't give everyone a million dollars. We are quick to ask why but the short answer is, He knows you wouldn't hold up your end of the deal. Honestly if you have the mindset of *"if I only had this, then I'd do this..."* then you aren't happy with what you do have and those who are good stewards of little will be given more.

MENTAL AND EMOTIONAL ABUSE

Mental and emotional abuse are different but go hand in hand. You start to believe you are worthless and you won't make it on your own without your abuser. They will feed you lies little by little until one day you wake up damaged and wonder how in the world it happened in the first place. Typically, the emotional abuse starts before the mental abuse takes place but it can happen the other way around as well.

Before me and my ex were engaged he picked up another woman to take her to an event that me and him used to attend together. This particular night he took her and beat around the bush telling me I had to drive myself. He sucked at communicating so I brushed it off as a communication issue at the time. Half way through this meeting he got up and left with the other women and didn't say anything to me. I kept thinking he showed her the bathroom or they got stuck talking to someone in the hall. But as time went on and on I got more and more heated. An hour later it was over, so I left and they were nowhere in sight. I called his phone back to back. Straight stalker mode. I know. It's slightly embarrassing admitting this but I was beyond mad and upset that he would do such a thing when we had marriage plans. So we were at a semi serious point in our relationship.

Anyway, after another hour went by, he finally answered the phone with the girl in the background. I was livid. I told him to meet me, I yelled at him and told him how wrong that was. I did all the things as if I was going to change him. Ha! A couple days later he came over to my place to "apologize" take note, this is where abuse happens. He apologized for *me* feeling the way I did. *Not for what he did.* Then proceeded to *warn* me that I *better* not yell at him like that again. I better not get mad at him like that again. I better not blow up his phone like that again. Ever, *or else* he wouldn't be able to handle it and he would snap on me.

Y'all he literally was threatening me to my face and I didn't take it seriously enough to leave then. He turned everything around on me and he accepted *my apology!* I only apologized for *yelling*. I should have expressed my emotions more calmly. I admitted *the way* I handled it was out of line. But I wasn't sorry for the way I felt. I had good reason to feel the way I did. We verbally laid out boundaries for us both not to be with the opposite sex alone and if it happens somehow we need to communicate with each other immediately. Yeah well, then after our engagement he told me how he was recently at her house with her mom and daughter having dinner and again shame on me for staying, but I had a group of church leaders who I trusted at the time encouraging me that these were not red flags, they were attacks from the enemy and I ought to forgive and stay with him. Abuse, abuse and more abuse and definitely gaslighting.

GASSLIGHTING

Gaslighting happened a whole lot in our relationship before and mostly during the marriage. I didn't know this term until my healing process after the divorce. Gaslighting is to manipulate (someone) using psychological methods into questioning their own sanity or powers of reasoning.

Another form of abuse I didn't know about at the time is verbal abuse. It is a range of words or behaviors used to manipulate, intimidate, and maintain power and control over someone. I share these with you so you know, and you can heal. If you're still with your abuser please take these seriously and get help. I included hotlines and resources so you can get the help you need now.

BREAKING FREE

The first part to healing is recognizing and acknowledging the abuse and trauma you faced (or are facing now) Take time to consider each type of abuse listed below and check off all that apply to you. Write down personal examples of each. Some may be more than you can count, so don't feel overwhelmed writing a whole book of examples. Just jot down one or two (or as many as you want).

Ask God to show you where and when you've been abused with each category. Even the abuse you may completely put off. For example, I use to always say I was never raped until God showed me the interactions that were actually considered rape. Once I acknowledged it, I was shocked to be honest but then I was able to get more healing in other areas tied to that.

- Emotional Abuse
- Mental Abuse
- Gaslighting
- Sexual abuse
- Rape
- Spiritual Abuse
- Financial Abuse
- Physical Abuse
- Verbal Abuse
- Bullying
- Trafficking
- Narcissistic Abuse
- Neglect
- Controlling
- Health Care Abuse
- Malpractice
- Medical Abuse

If you or your children are being abused, get help. Here's a 24 hour number you can call now 800-779-7233 or text the word START to the number 88788. You can also Google domestic violence help in the area you live.

3

Understanding Your True Identity

It wasn't until my ex husband grabbed my five-year old son by the throat, and threw him, that I finally had the courage to leave. If it weren't for that horrific moment, I think I would have stayed married, no matter what. I obviously didn't think he would hurt my children. But that's how it always is or else we wouldn't get in the relationship willingly, right?

I became too comfortable and lost all sense of my true identity and what God intended for me and my children and my whole lineage. I lost who I really was. I began to believe I was *just* his wife who was treated like a child, and I had to accept it. I believed God wasn't listening to my prayers about the marriage because this was my punishment and I deserved to be in this situation. I believed I would never amount to anything because I had no money and the little I had had to be spent before *asking* my "husband" for more to buy groceries or something for myself or the kids.

And yes, I used air quotes for the word "husband" because the way he treated me and my kids and our home and marriage was *not* what a husband is supposed to do. Husbands are to love their wives as Christ loves the church. Wives are supposed to submit to their husbands. As husband and wife, there are many other things we should do especially as being a Christian; but it's never supposed to bring our spouse harm or pain or fear or doubt. We both had the wrong idea of a submissive wife. That's for sure. When we face abuse and trauma we start to lose our identity. The more abuse, the more loss. But because *we* lose our identity doesn't mean the identity is gone. What is lost can be found. Lost doesn't mean vanished, or nonexistent. It just means misplaced.

You are not who your abuser says you are! You are not who or how your abuser makes you feel. You aren't even who *you* think you are. Your identity is not your social media following or lack thereof. It's not your home esthetic, career, bank account or title. And this is hard for most people to grasp because they give into an imposter mindset and rely on themselves and their accomplishments to prove to the world around them that they are someone *they think* everyone wants. When in reality we are exactly who God says we are, whether or not we believe it.

We all tend to have a bit, and others a lot, of this imposter mindset whether we know it or not; so let's work towards breaking that curse so you can live free in your true identity. Knowing your true identity will help you get out and stay out of abusive situations. When you know your true identity you can walk away from anything unapologetic. It may hurt but you'll heal faster. You'll walk with courage and your head held high. You'll apply for jobs you aren't qualified for on paper and get hired. You'll look at your bank account with no fear and no worry; because you know your Father and Maker of all things will never leave or forsake you. You will walk in wisdom and light, giving and not borrowing. You will do so many things you never thought possible and most importantly, you will help others along their journey to freedom. And I speak these things over you in Jesus' name.

Our true identity is found in Christ and in Christ alone. To all who receive Christ, He gave them the right to be children of God, to those who believe in His name, who were born, not of natural descent, or of the will of the flesh, or of the will of man, but of God.

If you are a child of God, then you're heirs—heirs of God
and fellow heirs with Christ. You are God's chosen one, holy
and beloved, with a compassionate heart, kindness,
humility, meekness, and patience. You are a chosen race, a
royal priesthood, a holy nation, a people for his possession,
so that you may proclaim the praises of The One who
called you out of darkness into His marvelous light.
The Lord who created you and formed you says, "Fear not
for I have redeemed you; I have called you by name, you
are Mine"

He chose you and appointed you so that you should go
and bear fruit. And whatever you ask the Father in Jesus
name, He may give it to you. Your citizenship is in heaven.
He has blessed you in Christ with every spiritual blessing in
the heavenly places. You have boldness and access with
confidence through your faith in Him. Since you have been
justified by faith, you have peace with God through Jesus
Christ. God will supply every need of yours according to His
riches in glory in Christ Jesus.

You have obtained an inheritance. You were predestined
according to the purpose of Him who works all things
according to the counsel of His will. It is God who

establishes you in Christ, and He has anointed you, and has also put His seal on you and given you His Spirit in your heart as a guarantee. The Lord is your shepherd. He makes you lie down in green pastures. He leads you beside still waters. He restores your soul. He leads you in paths of righteousness for His name's sake. Even though you walk through the valley of the shadow of death, you will fear no evil, because God is with you; His rod and His staff, *comfort* you.

God prepares a table before you in the presence of your enemies; and He anoints your head with oil. Your cup overflows because He gives you so much. You are more than a conqueror. God gave you a spirit of power and love and self-control; not fear. He predestined you for adoption to Himself as a daughter through His glorious grace, with which He has blessed you in the Beloved. In Him you have redemption through His blood, the forgiveness of your trespasses, according to the riches of His grace, which He lavished upon you, in all wisdom and insight.

"When you pass through the waters, I will be with you, and the rivers will not overwhelm you. When you walk through the fire, you will not be scorched, and the flame will not burn you." Says The Lord. "Because you are precious in my sight and honored, and I love you," says The Lord.

"Therefore I (Jesus) tell you, everything that you pray and ask for — believe that you have received it and it will be yours." You are like a tree planted beside flowing streams that bears its fruit in its season, and its leaf does not wither. Whatever you do prospers.

This and so many more all throughout scripture! So hold onto these truths, and apply them to your life daily! Never forget them!

Each of these scriptures I included, in order as I wrote them, in the back of this book for you so you can go read them from the Bible for yourself and see how they are true about all who have accepted Christ as Lord and Savior and love Him and are called to His will. Even if you haven't accepted Christ yet, these things are your true identity. God wants you to walk in your true identity. When you receive Him can you access all the gifts and spiritual blessings He has for you.

How amazing is it that we are these things! We walk around and don't even know it. We walk past others and they don't even know the potential. We were created for so much more than we are now and so much more than we can think or imagine. And that goes for everyone who is apart from Christ, just came to Christ, and those who have been steadily walking with Christ for years! You don't have to believe it or feel like it, just *know* that you are! This is your true identity. Now walk in that identity.

Your sins are washed away when you come to Christ and repent in your heart and God opens doors for you no man could open on his own and no man can shut! You are blessed and anointed!

No matter the situation you went through or are currently going through. Hold onto the hem of Jesus and let Him guide you. Pray at all times and thank God always. Let Him do a work in you.

Understanding your true identity sets you up for healing because when you know who you are, you won't allow the lies of others or the lies of your own thinking to affect you. Someone can tell you *"You'll never make it on your own if you leave me"* and you'll know that's a lie and it won't bother you as much because you know God is always with you and you can do all things through Christ who strengthens you. You'll be able to stop the lies immediately and not even let them take up space in your mind because you know God has already called you chosen and tells you that whatever you ask in His name it will be given to you. Therefore, you can leave a relationship or friendship and know everything will be okay because He always provides. He is the ultimate Provider.

Your true identity brings healing to areas of your life that have tormented you for years. It's the same thing. You start to recognize that you're not just some unemployed worthless single mom who can hardly keep a roof over your kids heads, because God has blessed you with all spiritual blessings and God will supply all your needs. He's your provider and protector and loves you more than a mother loves her newborn baby. And that love is indescribable.

Had I not kept my relationship with God, even though I started to believe my prayers weren't going to be answered, then when the physical child abuse happened to my son, I might have stayed married. And who knows what else would have happened. It was filling myself with God's word, and the Holy Spirit highlighting to me my true identity that made me have the courage to carefully seek help.

As much as I think back now and would have loved to have ended our marriage the second it happened, that wasn't my reality. I was terrified. I was terrified for myself and my children and the unborn twins I was carrying at the time. I was terrified child services would take my kids because we were married and I had nowhere to go. I was terrified that the church would disown me for even thinking of divorce, or worse, they would keep pushing me to stay with him. I had no money and I was about to have twins that were his. If we didn't stay married that meant he could get partial custody and then I would never know the abuse they would face until it was too late. A million thoughts ran through my mind at that moment and for the next couple of days after.

This is what happens when we lose our true identity. We don't think about all that God promises us and says about us. We don't think about time and time again in scriptures where He says He will protect us and He hears our prayers, reaches down from Heaven and grabs hold of us and pulls us out of the traps. We don't think about His unconditional love for us and how we can walk through the valley of the shadow of death and fear no evil because He guides and protects us. No fire will scorch us and no raging waters will drown us when we call out to Him for help. He is near the broken hearted and He hates abuse and evil.

So as I prayed and asked God what I was supposed to do He instantly reminded me of a dream I had two weeks prior.

Two weeks to the date I had a dream that warned me of this. The dream wasn't about abuse, but the Lord told me He was moving my due date up two weeks. When I woke up I checked my calendar and thought I'd miscarry my pregnancy or deliver too early. But I'd been praying and fasting for something to change in our marriage and I wanted God's will to be done. Those were the last words in complete surrender and desperation before I fell asleep and had that dream. The child abuse took place on that two week date. I *knew* this was my answer but I thought God hated divorce so much that He wouldn't dare allow something to happen that would lead to divorce.

I will never tell someone to divorce. But I will tell anyone that God hates abuse more than divorce and the idea that God hates divorce is usually taken out of context. I hate divorce too and although it was the best thing for me and my kids, it still makes me upset that I have that title now. Divorce itself is ugly, but God doesn't hate divorced individuals.

I don't know how many of you need to hear this but God still loves you and you will flourish and thrive, and there is still hope for you and a family with remarriage in God's timing. Forgive yourself for choosing your safety and your children's safety first. Forgive others for they know not what they say. And the hardest pill to swallow that we won't get into right this moment, forgive your abuser. It's for you. That calls for a couple deep breaths and a break.

Lord God help me to see myself the way You see me. Help me to love myself the way You love me and help me to forgive myself the way you call me to forgive. I want to walk in Your Will and I forgive myself for beating me up and thank You for always having Your just righteous hand on my life. Thank You for caring for me and our children. Thank You that You call me yours and I can come to You in times of heartache, brokenness, confusion, and desperation. Thank You for guiding me and walking with me. Thank You for making me lay down in green pastures and anointing my head with oil. Thank You that my cup overflows and You hear my cries. Thank You for the invite to the table that You have prepared for me in the presence of my enemies. In Jesus' Name Amen.

Because I knew my true identity I didn't entertain the *what if* thoughts in my mind. I knew my children needed to be safe and I was putting all my faith in God to provide for us a way out, as safe as possible and all that was to come after. I certainly had no idea all that was going to happen, but God was there every single step of the way showing me He had everything under control.

I'm not gonna lie. I had a lot of *sinking* moments where fear would creep in. Things got ugly and scary. I had to really rely on all 366 fear not commandments from the Lord. Court isn't fun. Police and investigators and state police and detectives and lawyers, attorneys, judges, and case workers, who all had the power to take my children, call me a liar, and whatever else they could do, made me fear a whole lot! But I chose every single day after every single phone call to stand on the promises of God and trust and put my faith in Him. The only One that mattered. I knew that if I remained faithful God would repay evil for me and bring justice to the just and righteous.

This is why knowing your true identity is so critical to learn. I could have let all the fearful bad thoughts consume me and give up, but I didn't. And neither do you. Even if the only thing you know about your true identity is what you just read in this chapter, that's honestly all you need to know right now. It was a lot that I went over so far and the Bible is filled with so much more. But take what you've read and write them down. Even if it's just two or three and read them daily. God will continue to show you who you are.

BREAKING FREE

Grab your journal and grab some sticky notes or post cards. You can even get a dry erase marker and write these on the mirrors in your house. We are going to start planting some seeds.

Write down at least two truths that I mentioned in this chapter and that stick out to you the most about your true identity in Christ. A bunch of Bible verses are in the back of this book or you can just go back into this chapter and grab some.

Once you write them in your journal AND on the sticky notes or mirror, I want you to memorize them. Say them to yourself every single day. Every time a bad thought pops in your head, *"I have redeemed you, you are mine" my cup overflows. He anoints my head with oil. I will walk and not*

*faint. I will soar on wings like eagles. The Lord is my
protector and provider.*

Write as many as you can. You can even write it in
paragraph form like I did or write the corresponding verse
with each truth. You can write it as if God is speaking to you
Himself or write it as you would say a prayer using the
words "I" to make it personalized to you. Or a combination
of all the ways you like.

I personally like doing them as a combination in paragraph
form like I did in the example above, and as a letter straight
from God like He is talking directly to me. But you do it
however you feel best for you. And read them, or the whole
paragraph or letter, every single day for at the very least 30
days.

Create a screen shot in your phone or background
wallpaper, you can write it in a blank card and set it on your
desk at work. Use a sticky note inside your car or locker.
However and wherever you can see it throughout the day.
And when you have those memorized, get more and
memorize a couple more for 30 more days.

Never stop doing this. This will be a continuous practice until you have them memorized and no longer need a daily visual in your face. Trust me, you will get to that point eventually. But it's no hurry, no rush, and it will only help. One day you will be asked how you're doing and instead of your auto response, "good" you will start answering with promises that encourage and uplift others. "Hey, How are you?" "I'm free!" "I'm filled with joy" Even if you still only say "good" they will see the light shining through you and know your meaning of good is legit.

4

PERMISSION TO FORGIVE YOURSELF

As soon as I heard a blood curtailing scream from my five-year old, I dropped my makeup and ran to him. My husband walked out of the room so casual as if nothing happened, as I dropped to my knees asking what happened. The terror in my sons' eyes and a bright red neck are engraved in my memory.

As he gasped for breath, holding his head with one hand and his shirt collar with the other, he finally got out the words "Daddy picked me up by my throat and he threw me."

Every emotion swelled up inside of me and all I could do was scream at my husband to tell me why he would do that. I held my son and examined him as my husband just nonchalantly claimed he didn't, at the time, and then went downstairs leaving us there in panic and fear. It was another "grab the life remote and hit rewind" moment. And still no remote to turn back the hands of time. What had been done was done.

I've watched enough movies to put my every move after, on guard. We had to go to church and I had no way of escaping at the very moment. Plus I was sure children and youth would take my kids from me if I reported right away since we lived together and were married. I was terrified. It was like walking on thin ice trying to plan every move perfectly or it would be the end. Not to mention who would actually help us. I had visions of him finding out we told someone and him coming home with his silencer and night vision on his big gun, that he adored so much, and killing us all.

The only words I could muster up to my son in that moment sounded so unhelpful and I can't even think of a better word to describe how inconsiderate I must have sounded to my son, when I asked, "Can you forgive him?" Of course my son said, "no" and I just held him and told him that's okay, we could work on it together.

Forgiving my husband at the time was not anything I would have ever thought up on my own and it was never meant for a reconciliation. I truly believe this was the Holy Spirit working in me to begin the long hard process of forgiveness.

Forgiveness is something much more than saying "everything is okay, don't worry about everything you did and all the hurt you've caused me. Yeah we can live together as if nothing happened now and all is good." Forgiveness is not forgetting. Although I'll be the first to admit that every time I think of forgiving I always think of forgetting first. I have to repeatedly remind myself that that's not actual forgiveness.

Forgiveness to many is a hard core curse word that should never be spoken, but I promise you if you keep that mindset you will start to cause your own wounds; and no matter if you believe it or not you'll be away from Christ for eternity because you won't be forgiven yourself. And that's not to say the abuse, trauma, pain and wrongdoings done *to* you were at all your fault; but I'm talking about the things that we need forgiveness from in all other areas of our lives.

"If you forgive others their trespasses, your heavenly Father will also forgive you, but if you do not forgive others their trespasses, neither will your Father forgive your trespasses." (Matthew 6:14-15)

Just a quick google search says, "Psychologists generally define forgiveness as a conscious, deliberate decision to release feelings of resentment or vengeance toward a person or group who has harmed you, regardless of whether they actually deserve your forgiveness."

To me this makes more sense than the made-up definition equating to forgetting. Like I can actually forgive. JustDisciple.com explains biblical forgiveness perfectly. It reads, "Biblical forgiveness is the process of forgiving someone or being forgiven as illustrated in the Bible. Forgiveness itself is defined as the letting go of sin. In the Bible, this includes forgiving everyone, every time, of everything, as an act of obedience and gratefulness to God. It acknowledges the sacrifice God made through His Son Jesus who died to restore the relationship between God and man.

Forgiveness does not mean excusing, forgetting, permitting repetition of the sinful act against you, or guaranteeing reconciliation with the perpetrator.

Okay now we're taking a load off our shoulders. Was it just me? But that made me breathe easy. Scientifically and biblically forgiveness is clearly about the one doing the forgiving. You are letting resentment and anger go from yourself. You're kicking it out of your house, your body, your temple, your life. You're stepping off the judge's seat and allowing God to be God. You're walking away from your abuser saying "you no longer have control over me. You no longer have control over my mind and thoughts. I no longer will let the lies you made me believe continue to infect me. I no longer am going to stay up all night angry and upset with you about all the affairs you've had. Yeah you controlled me during our marriage but you will no longer control me.

I'm moving forward. I'm trusting in The Lord to do with you as *He* sees fit. Besides, He can punish you more than I ever could. And for your sake I pray He has mercy on you. Why? Because Christ didn't just die for me but for you too. Will I let you hurt me again? Absolutely not! Why? Because I know who I am and I know who my Father is. And I know how He handles the righteous who obey and those who disobey. I'm not righteous to stay out of trouble, I'm righteous because I love the Lord with all my heart, mind and soul. And I can forgive you for destroying years of my life, stealing chapters of my life and demolishing my self worth, self esteem and identity. I can forgive you because I don't deserve to be bound any more. I forgive you because I know my true identity and I won't let you stand in the way of that any longer. I forgive you because bitterness and anger will only shorten my life. I forgive you because I need to heal. I forgive you because Christ forgave me. I forgive you because I deserve to be set free."

When you can get out of God's way and let Him take the wheel, let Him take the judge's seat, let Him do what He does best, you will find what it means to be made to lie down in green pastures. You can put your trust in God because He is the maker and finisher. He wants you to live in joy and freedom. You will never know true freedom until you break the chains of resentment.

Trust me, your abuser is not going to be walking around living their best life and not have to pay for their abuse to you just because *you* forgive them. God is a just God and vengeance is His. God will repay evil for evil. We don't have to. I strongly encourage you to practice forgiveness daily. It doesn't happen like a flip of a switch, 99 percent of the time. And if it does then praise God! But don't get discouraged if you feel it's taking you months or years or decades to forgive. I do strongly suggest you also seek wise counsel and prayer to help you forgive especially in harder circumstances. Most of us will need to break soul ties first before forgiveness. I had to do this several times.

As I'm writing this book I am still working on forgiving my ex husband. I choose to forgive daily, especially with this book as my testimony of that marriage and abuse. It brings up a lot of memories. I've cried multiple times writing this.

So for me to ask my son if he could forgive during the most traumatic experience of his life was a direct result of my acknowledgment of who God is and what Christ did for us on the cross. I didn't understand it then, but the more I knew Him, the more I knew me; and the more I got closer to Him, the more He showed me. Trust in the Lord with all your heart and lean not on your own understanding; in all your ways acknowledge him, and he will make your paths straight.

Forgiveness

does not mean excusing, forgetting, permitting repetition of the sinful act against you, or guaranteeing reconciliation with the perpetrator.

Grab your journal and get ready to write. First write down the definitions of forgiveness. You can write word for word the definitions I gave you in this chapter.

Now which part of the definition sticks out to you the most? Which part was eye opening or a tough pill to swallow? Underline that part.

Then highlight the part of the definition that you needed to hear. It may be the same part or not but you should have something underlined *and* something highlighted.

Now take some time to write down your forgiveness letter for your abuser, but to yourself. This will hit triggers. This will sting, burn and hurt. This will feel impossible. It's okay to cry. Keep reading the biblical definition of forgiveness that you wrote down. Remember, forgiveness is releasing *your* resentment.

You can keep writing to God once you finish your letter or just start praying if your hand hurts, and let God comfort you.

Daughter, I hear you and I love you. I am so sorry you went through all that you did. I am so sorry our children went through the evil that was done to them. Let me be your shepherd. Let me lead you. Let me heal you. Let me set your feet on solid ground. I will restore your health, and all that was stolen and lost. Do not fear, for I am with you; do not be afraid, for I am your God. I will strengthen you; I will help you; I will hold on to you with my righteous right hand. I will guide you on paths you have not known and turn darkness into light in front of you. Do not remember the past events; pay no attention to things of old. Look, I am about to do something new; even now it is coming. Do you not see it? For my plans are to prosper you. I have made a way, because I love you.

BREAKING FREE PART 2

I pray you already feel the chains come loose and hit the ground from the first forgiveness exercise. If you don't, don't worry. Again it takes time and no one seems to talk about this second part to forgiveness which is just as critical as forgiving others.

FORGIVING YOURSELF

Not for what they did to you but what you're doing to yourself. Stop blaming yourself for things you can't change and definitely stop blaming yourself for the things you had absolutely no say or part in. Forgive yourself for trying too hard, not trying enough, or trying the "wrong" things. Forgive yourself for listening to others instead of your own intuition, the Holy Spirit, or paying attention to the red flags. Forgive yourself for calling yourself names. You're not a moron, you aren't stupid, you're not an idiot. Forgive yourself for thinking you have bad judgment. You're not gullible. You're not crazy.

It's not your fault he hit you. It's not your fault he left with another woman. It's not your fault he harmed your children. It's not your fault he spit on you. It's not your fault he smashed your phone and beat your face in. It's not your fault you were trapped and left for dead. It's not your fault that your children were sold into pornography. It's not your fault you got drugged and molested countless times. It's not your fault your husband cut you off from your family and friends. It's not your fault your husband raped you. It's not your fault your mom let your dad rape you. It's not your fault your mom didn't love you. It's not your fault your dad walked away. It's not your fault they stole you. It's not your fault they tricked you into believing all the lies. It's not your fault you fell for it. It's not your fault you stayed. It's not your fault you were too afraid to speak up against your abuser(s).

It's not your fault that all your relationships turn to abuse. It's not your fault you couldn't take it anymore. It's not your fault you decided you needed better. It's not your fault your family and home are broken. It's not your fault your children will never see their abusive relative again. Forgive yourself for sleeping with the wrong person and having your children. Forgive yourself for not choosing adoption. Forgive yourself for choosing adoption. Forgive yourself for the abortion. Forgive yourself for the miscarriage. Forgive yourself for your baby's SIDS. Forgive yourself for your child's death. It's not your fault that you're depressed and suicidal.

Forgive yourself. Forgive yourself. Forgive yourself.

When you ask God to forgive you, He does. You can't keep yourself in bondage. It's not your fault. You're not responsible for someone else's actions toward you. Stop letting the spirit of *but if I only* take over your life. We can always learn from our mistakes and I highly recommend we all learn from ourselves and each other. But you can't beat yourself up drowning in the thoughts of *if only I'd told someone. If I only left sooner. If only I didn't care what others thought. But if I only ran away. But if I only fought back. If I only learned my lesson. If I only.. if I only.. if I only..* You can fill in plenty I'm sure.

I battled this from the time of our wedding day before we even said our I dos, the entire marriage, and a whole year after our divorce. Sometimes the, *if I onlys*, still try to sneak up on me and bring me back to a dark place but I refuse to entertain the thoughts. As should you. The more I stop the thoughts in their tracks the faster they go away and the less they happen. Knowing who you are and who you belong to along with forgiving yourself are all part of this beautiful crazy journey to healing. *If I onlys* will robe you of your peace, joy and freedom.

Keep hold of your true identity, forgive, heal and grow. And when you've come to some peace with forgiving yourself, circle back around to forgiving others. Then circle back around to forgive yourself. It's a cycle that may take many rounds and that's okay. God honors the very fact that you're trying.

Ask God for help, ask a leader at your church for help, ask a trusted accountability partner for help. If you have no one to turn to, Facebook has many groups for women who need healing and all kinds of other support groups. You'll have to weed out the naysayers, and if they aren't making you feel supported then get out of the group. Unfortunately there are many groups that are advertised as good but they are filled with hate and condemnation. Also google support groups in your area or local church communities. Seek counseling for yourself. They have them on your phone now where you have access to a professional licensed counselor all via text, video chat or phone call. Some churches also have classes and support groups. While you're looking and waiting, always always, always talk to God.

Remember who you are and whose you are. You are the daughter of the Most High King who reigns forever and ever. Who sits enthroned forever and ever. Who has dominion over everything seen and unseen. He knows your deepest thoughts. He knit you together. Every cell, organ, fiber, hair, every dream and purpose in your life He gave you. It's His breath that fills your lungs. His grace and mercy and unconditional *never-ending-far-as the-East-is-from-the-West* love that can not be taken from you! He forgives you. He washes you clean and puts a robe around you. He calls you by name. He says you are mine!

You are mine says The Lord. You will never be left, you will never be alone. I know you feel it. I know you don't understand but I have a plan for you. I am taking your pain and turning it into something good, something amazing, something beautiful. You are the answer. Your are precious. I delight in you. You are Mine daughter. I delight in you. You are Mine. You are Mine. I remove the chaos. I give you My perfect peace. Shalom Shalom. I remove your transgressions. I trample your enemy. I give you victory. I give you My peace. Shalom Shalom. You don't have to perform for My love. You don't have to perform for My goodness. I freely give it to you because I love you. Yes it's that simple. Yes. Yes you will be whole again. Yes I make you whole; yes I heal. I'm doing a new thing in you; can't you see it? Yes I was there and yes I wept with you. Yes it broke my heart too. No you couldn't have done anything more than come to Me. Yes I am taking care of it. Yes justice will be served. Yes vengeance is mine. No daughter, you rest. Forgive yourself the way I forgave you. Yes I already forgave you. No, my precious, you didn't have to ask. Because I love you. You don't have to pretend anymore, you don't have to put on a fake smile anymore. You don't have to try. Let Me take care of it. Let Me do it, Let Me heal you. Let me send justice. Let me finish what I've started. Take hold of My hand. I'll never let you go. I'll never let you go. It's okay. I've got you. I'm not going anywhere *daughter. You are Mine. I love you. Rest. Trust Me. Have a little faith in Me. I am increasing your faith right now. I'm stirring your heart. That's Me knocking. That's My peace. That's My comfort. Do I make mistakes? You're no mistake. You were made in perfect love and in Our image. How could We have made a mistake? You are formed by and created for Me, the Son and the Holy Spirit. You are Mine daughter. I make no mistake. Can I take over for you? Can I fight this fight for you now? Can you trust Me to do what I do best? Can you forgive yourself for My name's sake? Can you accept this gift from My hand I freely give to you? You are so beautiful and I LOVE YOU.*

5

Escaping Trauma

Escaping your abuser is hard enough as it is. But once we really start believing God, what He says about us and who we are; we will be able to stop believing all the lies and leave our abuser.

For some of us it looks like packing up your things and secretly going to a relative's house. Or taking an overnight bag with essentials and fleeing to another state. It may look like getting a protection from abuse (PFA) order from the judge and having the court system help you find shelter or evict your abuser from the home. For some of us it requires law enforcement to find us and arrest our abuser, bringing us into safety and reuniting us with our family we were taken from.

Escaping may take you a week, months, or years. Some of you are still waiting for escape and rescue. I'm praying for you! When we escape we feel free, at first thanking God we made it out alive. Like a bird that's been set free from a cage, a lion that's been set free from a tiny zoo enclosure or circus, or a beached whale that was helped back into the ocean.

Then the chains grip you up again and just like the Israelites in the wilderness you begin to realize it was easier in bondage. It was easier when you at least had a roof over your head and food to eat. You start thinking of all the good times and completely ignore all the abuse you became used to, to justify a reason for going back. This is because we now have to escape our trauma.

In case you're not familiar with the history of the Israelites, I'm going to give you a brief overview using my child-story-retelling skills. My nieces and nephews love when I retell a story.

So in the land of Egypt, long ago, there were people called the Israelites. The Pharaoh feared them saying "Oh no, they will all realize how horrible I am and take me out one day so I must use my pea sized brain and put an end to that happening because of course I'm greater than their God!" So he forced them to be slaves. Now he owns them and they fear him and rely on him for work, food and shelter for their families. They are stuck. Trapped. And completely dependent upon the enemy. They lost all identity of who they were and who their God is. (Or else they would have done exactly what the Pharaoh feared and overtook him) *Sounds all too familiar to me.*

Then Pharaoh being a pea brain, hears of a new king that will rule over him. And afraid of babies he demands all baby boys under the age of 2 be killed. He just couldn't imagine having to bow down to a king in diapers. *All jokes aside he's sick for that for real!* Back to the story. One of God's faithful, brave Israelite woman decided to put her baby boy in a basket and send him down the river when she couldn't hide him any more. And what do you know!? He ends up in the hands of Pharaoh's daughter who wants to keep him and names him *dun dun dun...* Moses! God really just put one of His people right in the enemy's house. Check mate! Moses grows up and has a light bulb moment one day when he sees an Egyptian beating on his people. Moses goes to help and ends up killing the Egyptian puppet, we'll call him.

So to speed up the story, Moses runs away, God sends him back, God turns Pharaoh's world upside down sending plague after plague; killing his first born son, and all the others who didn't have the lamb's blood over their doors which is where we get Passover from. Finally, Pharoah pea brain gives in to God. About time! And lets all the Israelites free. They all leave happy and excited they are no longer slaves, they see signs and wonders from God during their journey, and then they start to get antsy because the trip to their promised land flowing with milk and honey. *Yours might look like 100 acres in the beautiful mountains or a million dollar home with a private oceanfront or penthouse in Dubai or a villa in the Costa Rica.* You get the point. So they complain and want to go back.

They'd rather go back to what was familiar to them than trust God and the goodness He has promised them. In doing this they turned what could have been a few days into 40 whole years! Don't fall into the trap of going back to what's familiar.

Don't allow yourself to grow weary in the fight for your life. Trust me I know how hard it is. And yes I know I could have had it worse, but what has happened to me personally has been the worse that has ever happened to me. I would never have imagined. Looking back now I can't even believe I went through the things I did. Losing my son and the way it happened was horrific for me. Just like the marriage I was in. Another horrific chunk of my life scorched. And to have to live with the fact I chose to marry someone that abused my kids and took part of their childhood, that they have to live with for the rest of their lives was torture on my soul. I know you can relate to those feelings in your life. We can never compare our worst days with someone else's worst days. The worse that has happened to you is real and caused real lasting pain and trauma. You have to remove the mindset of, "but others have been through worse" and acknowledge every emotion and trigger it has caused you. That way you can work through it and heal properly.

I don't want to give you a bandage and pain meds to cover up the deep wounds in your heart. I want God to sedate you, cut you open, remove the infection, stitch you back together and let you recover so you are fully healed from the inside out! Sounds painful I know. But healing isn't a pretty word. And only those who have to heal understand that. Which is why I am helping you walk through this now. I told you in the beginning, I'm here to help you the *whole* way through. Escaping our abuser now sounds a whole lot easier once it's done and you're faced with a taunting giant named trauma.

Don't allow
yourself to grow
weary in the

fight

for your Life

Trauma is the *lasting* emotional response that often results from living through a distressing event. Long after the traumatic event occurs, people with trauma can often feel shame, helplessness, powerlessness and intense fear. Disturbing and distressing experiences include domestic violence, death of a loved one, natural disaster, war, or the result of a physical injury. It can be a single incident, repeated or a combination of different experiences piling up.

We can look at trauma in the physical or spiritual. Whichever is easier for you to identify with, so we can get rid of its lasting eternal damage it's causing us. Shame we covered pretty much in the chapter of forgiveness. Forgiving ourselves for what we did, didn't do, and our *if I only* thoughts.

Shame

Shame is the painful emotion caused by a consciousness of guilt, failure or impropriety. Shame often results in the paralyzing conviction and or belief that you are worthless and of no value to others or God. But God says whoever believes in Him shall not be put to shame. You don't have to feel shame because of what happened to you. Let the shame go.

Helplessness

Helplessness is not being able to help yourself. Don't let that consume you either. There is help out there. You may not be able to help yourself in many many situations, but help *is* out there *for you*. Remember this when we are letting go of trauma; trauma is *feeling* helpless. Let that thought go. You *feel* helpless. But you're not! Go get help from the court and law enforcement, get help from the state and government, get help from the food banks, local churches, your community. There are many resources for you. Google will become your best friend. Don't be afraid to speak up and just ask someone if they know of a place for whatever help it is you need. Lose the shame, don't believe in being helpless. Although you're not the one keeping your abuser away, paying your rent, or buying your vehicle, you are allowing others to help you and that *is* helping yourself.

I know for many of us the sound of asking law *enforcement* for help is triggering. I'll be honest it kinda stung my heart when I felt the Lord edit that sentence to include it. I've gone to law enforcement for serious help and they let me and my kids down multiple times. Once children and youth finished their investigation for the child abuse cases, I thought the detectives would help carry out some more legal actions so we could get a sense of justice for what my ex-husband had done. The detective working our case over the phone sounded like he cared. But when we met in person he didn't seem like he had any experience with children and his coffee was getting cold if you catch my drift. I got a phone call from him a few days later and he said they weren't pressing charges because my 5-year-old was too afraid to talk to him so good luck. And he left it at that. Very cold and no help. The child abuse findings still held so that made me feel better at least and the PFA stayed in place. To me that showed someone at least cared about us and wanted to help.

I didn't grow a bitter heart towards law enforcement, and I still don't. My ex-husband then violated his PFA at the courthouse! Seconds after the judge told him the consequences for even speaking to me. I reported it immediately and the judge let him go. Then my ex spotted us on the highway. Slowed down his truck until I had no choice but to pass him and he looked in my van, saw me and all four kids, the twin newborn babies included, and then proceeded to follow me. I took an exit and in my rear view mirror I saw him speed up and cut off the car behind me and he almost ran me off the road. It happened so fast and I was so scared I couldn't even let out a sound. I just held my breath waiting to flip in a ditch. By the grace of God we were not hit so I took another exit as quickly as I could without a turn signal at the last possible second to prevent him from trying anymore crazy stunts. My daughter had it on video the whole time and when I called law enforcement once I was safely off the road, they told me over the phone there's nothing they can do about it. I reminded them of the PFA. Protection from abuse because abuse had already happened, meaning he is at risk of abusing again and they still wouldn't help. I called my attorney and she told me I had to call the police.

I know this part of the story isn't the most helpful right now if you're considering getting a PFA or not. Go get one! That's not where the story ends. We did eventually get more help than I ever thought possible and I thank God for that and the strength to not give up. That's just one of the parts that I share with you because I do understand that hearing, "get help from law enforcement" can trigger bad for you. I never gave up though. Just because one person who doesn't care that day, doesn't mean they all don't care. And when we give up, it makes more and more not care about the ones who truly need it. So don't give up for yourself, your children, or the other women and children who really do need it. (And men I know some men who actually need help from abusive women) Trust in the Lord and you will not grow weary or weak. He will give you strength.

Powerlessness

Powerlessness is a lack of authority. You're not being heard. As a single mom I can *feel* like this multiple times when I'm telling my kids over and over again to stop doing something. Why do I have to keep repeating myself? But in terms of trauma, it's much deeper.

In my marriage I had absolutely no say when it came to anything he disagreed with me on. If he made up his mind about my kids, school, work, holidays, all my words, feelings and emotions were completely ignored and I'm not exaggerating whatsoever. I know many of you can relate. When we are free and trying to break the bonds of trauma we have this feeling like although we are free from the abuse, we are still trapped. The judge overlooks us and lawyers think we'll eventually go back so why bother with us. We feel like our voice is silenced and no one understands. Our family and friends turn their backs on us and our abusers' family and friends think we're crazy. No one hears us and there is nothing we can do. This puts us in a dangerous spot of giving up or giving in if we don't harness our frustration and pain to properly give us the strength we need to press through.

We can get upset and mad and frustrated and irritated and sad and give up completely turning from help, healing, and even God. Or we end up giving in and letting the abuser say and do what they want and dropping everything. Some even go back to the abuser because they think *I'm not heard now. I get no help so I might as well go back and not be heard, least I have a roof over my head and someone to call a friend.* Nooo Girl noooo. You are heard!

You are heard by your father in Heaven and He will never leave or forsake you. "I called to the Lord in my distress, and I cried to my God for help. From his temple he heard my voice, and my cry to him reached his ears."

Intense Fear

Intense fear is last on the list of feelings we live with after the effects of trauma that we must escape from. Fear in itself is bad enough. Add intensity to it and we're talking about a serious battle. But you can win this and escape. I'm no doctor or scientist but doing my own research and comparing what I've found on fear and the effects it has on your body, it's makes sense why God tells us not to fear so many times in the Bible.

Fear has physical effects on our body. When you are in fear your brain releases a stress hormone that increases your blood pressure and heart rate. The blood flow in your body starts to move *away* from your heart and into your limbs. Endorphins are released and you go into a fight or flight mode. Which makes sense to me why the blood flow goes to your limbs. You're either swinging in a fight or getting up and running. Because of all this it causes arrhythmias which is where the phrase "my heart skipped a beat" comes from. It does. And it could cause heart attacks.

Being in a state of fear constantly is where anxiety lives. And it's not good for your mental or physical health. You can't think or focus clearly which can result in poor choices as small as forgetting appointments and deadlines, to getting into car accidents. You hear it all the time how a car came out of nowhere. In reality the car was always there, and yes it may have been speeding, but it didn't come out of nowhere. It's like your brain is in snapshot mode working through AOL dial up and the rest of the world is live and has high speed internet. Fear, and anger I just wanna add, is stored in your spine.

Again, for me it makes perfect sense because my back and shoulders are always the first thing I tell any massage therapist to work on the longest. Now of course yes there are many other factors to heart attacks and back pains but the point is that when you hear the term "fear is crippling," it's for a reason.

The good news is, we get to escape from all these things. Talking with God and reading His word are always number one on my list! They work. But it's not the *only* thing you can do. So *while* you're talking to God and reading His word consider these as well.

Friends and family

Getting godly counsel from someone else is a huge part of healing and escaping trauma as well. You can always start with a trusted non judgmental friend or family member but don't fully rely on family or friends to get you through. My dad is a huge help for me. He is a believer and he always has a positive outlook. So talking with him has become very easy. However, he's my dad so when I tell him things of course they upset him. We both also talk with my aunt who lives on the other side of the country. She too is a believer and she is a great person to talk to, she has a beautiful testimony as well, and I always know she will pray and she will be honest with me.

Professional counsel

Seek counseling from a local church or a therapist. Even if it isn't Christian based as long as they are a professional in abuse, narcissistic abuse, trauma, ptsd, triggers and whatever specific traumas you're needing to break free from. I had sessions with a counselor at my church that was able to help me dig in deep and release ties and bonds related to my childhood as well as the divorce. Professionals are trained to help and of course you always learn something new and as long as you apply all you've learned, you are taking more steps into your healing. TalkSpace and Better Health are just a couple online therapists whose apps can be downloaded. They are not a sponsor so I don't have a discount code but maybe by the time of publishing I'll edit to add one.

Support groups

Support groups are often free but some come with a small fee depending on the group. Facebook support groups are free and can be very helpful! You can even find coaching within these groups and books and courses and other helpful resources. I think these just speak for themselves. Some sound better than they actually are but join a few and you'll find one or two you love and you can always leave the groups, no questions asked. I personally like the private groups and you can see if anyone on your friends list is in the group so you can almost hide. And now you can post comments anonymously in case you just want to ask or vent completely private.

Journaling

This one hits home for me big time. My journals are so important to me. And not to remember the past, but I love to go back each year and see where I've come from and I always find good words of wisdom I've forgotten that help me with my current situation. If your journal turns out as one you don't want to remember at all then after it's full you can always thank God for what He's brought you through and then burn it. Journaling every day takes a lot off my shoulders even when I'm not struggling with anything in particular. I'll go to my journal just to write down every thought in my head, so I can go to sleep, or I'll write until I fall asleep. When I am upset, stressed or angry, I turn to my journal. I have a journal for each year. You may need a journal for each month and that's perfectly okay, and great actually. You can use this journaling time to talk to God as well. I spill out everything in my mind and then start adding prayer requests, and then back to dumping my feelings and writing down words, verses or songs that pop into my mind; and I can go back when I'm done and look them up.

Keeping a record

This is not to go against the Bible, keep *no record of wrong*. This is a different record. You should keep it separate from your journal, but if you want it all in one place then highlight or mark your record pages for easy access; because you will need to reflect and adjust accordingly. Record what triggers you. Maybe you're upset more than usual. Almost back in your depressed state of mind. What did you do today? You may have watched a romantic comedy and the romance triggered you. Or the *one* sideways joke that was said in the movie to be funny that gave you a flashback. It may have been a conversation you overheard from someone in the next aisle at the store or a radio ad. This may take a lot of digging at first but the more you recognize your triggers, the faster you will know and then we can work through them.

Work through triggers

The best way to work through a trigger is prayer. Even if you just started your walk with Christ, or not sure if you want to yet. Or you don't know if you want to at all. Prayer works. You have nothing to lose when you pray to God in Jesus' name and it won't hurt you, so you could at least give it a try. Give yourself time to heal. This may look different for every person, but if you know tv shows and movies trigger you, stay off the tv for a while. This was *Definitely me.* It took me over a year after leaving my ex husband to finally watch tv again and especially anything remotely romantic. Talk to a trustworthy friend. And when it comes to triggers this is one time you may want to start with a friend that will just be there for you and not try to tell you what you should do. Unless you're ready to ask them their opinion. Don't wait too long for that though. If you are triggered by something and talk to a friend today and tomorrow or this week and next week, the third conversation you should start asking for a little of their opinion. Their honesty may sound harsh to you at first and even set you off again, but that's why it's important to pick a trustworthy friend, or family member, to do this with; so you can remind yourself later that they always have your back and you know they want what's best for you.

Forgiveness

We talked about this in an earlier chapter but forgiveness is huge. Forgive yourself and those who have hurt you. Go back and read that chapter again. Forgiveness is the most important and *usually* the longest to achieve but it's possible and can be done.

Honesty

Be open and honest with yourself and whoever you're seeking help from. If you can't be honest with yourself about your emotions then you won't heal. The truth shall set you *free.* If you feel angry, feel angry. Just don't do anything that would harm you or others. Don't feel angry and drink a bottle of wine, or slash someone's tires. If you feel sad, allow yourself to feel sad for a day, week or a couple months. It took me years when I lost my son. And while you're feeling your emotions, give them to God and ask Him for help. Tell Him everything on your mind and ask Him to help you. He will. We don't always want to walk around telling any and everyone our business, but if it's someone you can be even a little bit honest with, then do so when they ask how you're doing.

Just responding "I've had better days" releases chains because when we keep saying "I'm good" we are coming into agreement with the chaos, hurt and trauma in our lives. Don't come into agreement with the devil, that's how I like to look at it. Plus you never know who you're being honest with. God may give them a direct message for you at that very moment, or a hug or resource you need. You may even allow that person to feel safe enough to come out and say "you know I'm not doing good either, I just buried my 2-year old," and then *you* can be a comfort or answered prayer for that person. And when we are a comfort to others it releases strongholds on us.

If you're ever feeling down, go help someone else. Make someone else smile. Watch what it does for you. I do this a lot with prayer requests. After I did what I could to help myself, I found prayer request chains; usually on Facebook, and I start praying for every single person who commented. They don't know but I do, and I start feeling better enough to get myself back up and keep fighting my personal battles.

Make your home your sanctuary. A safe place. A comfortable place where the Holy Spirit dwells and you feel at peace. Clean and organize. Declutter and throw away everything with no purpose or holds a bad memory. Throw away the old toys. You know the kids get more every year for birthdays and holidays and in between. Donate the clothes that don't fit anymore. Buy a size or two up if you need it. Even if you're actively working out. Be comfortable in what you're wearing. Throw out or donate all the, *I might need this one day,* things. If you haven't used it all year, you don't need it.

Buy something new to freshen up the place. Thrift stores have lots of good finds. And places like Marshall's and Burlington always have the cutest stuff in season and trend if you like a good deal. I did all these things and now it's such a habit I still keep my house organized. And when it starts to clutter up with the kids' clothes they've outgrown; and I find more things I don't want or need anymore, and I get it out of my house. Clutter throws me off track. I absolutely love to organize everything! My fridge is a 'TikTok organize with me fridge.' The kids' dressers, our closets, and the whole house I like to keep organized. My mom has said it's unhealthy in a joking way just because of how organized it is. And it used to bother me when one thing was out of place. Over the time of healing, I've gotten more lenient and now things can be out of place without triggering me, but I still keep it all organized. And now I have a healthy balance.

Love

Love yourself. Practice good healthy habits that will improve your self esteem, character, mindset and life. Start saving money, making more money, washing your face before bed, buy skin care products and use them daily. Learn a new skill, workout, meal plan; read helpful books, *like this one and share it,* meet new people, go out on the town. Really love yourself. Don't forget all those sticky notes about your true identity.

Love others. Donate your money or time to charities, soup kitchens, hospitals. You can love others every single day by smiling and erasing what your parents engraved in your minds as a child, "stranger danger." Say "Hi" to people when you walk past them. Pay for someone's coffee if they are in line behind you. Or their groceries. My biggest joy is blessing others with groceries when they least expect it. I try to do it 100% anonymously, but I've been behind people who have to ask the cashier to put things back and I just buy it for them and they light up like they just saw an angel. And I do believe what they are spiritually seeing, when they physically look at me, is Christ in me.

These things start to regain your confidence and reset your mindset to thinking and believing and becoming a new person. *You have turned my mourning into dancing; You have put off my sackcloth and clothed me with gladness (Psalm 30:11).* You are not forgetting your past, you are healing and moving forward so that you can help others who need you.

BREAKING FREE

Keeping in mind everything you learned from the previous chapters and this one, grab your journal and make a daily to do list. Take your time with this one and be as realistic as possible with your current situation and life circumstances. The point of this is not to get elaborate and then look back later and see a list of unaccomplished goals and feel like a failure. Even if it's just *one* thing. It's a huge success and step in your healing process.

Write down one thing you can do every single day to help in your escape from trauma and healing. It may only be to smile at a stranger. Or do your hair. For some it may be to just get out of the bed. Read a book. Maybe your one and only thing is to cut out sweets. Journal. Read one verse from the Bible. Make your bed, put away laundry, run the vacuum before bed, clean the kitchen table every morning. Turn on worship music as soon as you wake up and let it play all day. Maybe your one thing is to start therapy. Take a walk. Pray for someone else, declutter a room, closet or that one junk drawer. Actually eat a meal. Or three every day.

When you are getting good and comfortable with one, add another. This is why I say it may take time and be realistic. Some of us can add five things to our list right now and some may only be able to manage one thing right now. When it's time to add some more you may be able to add three more things, ten more things or just one. Don't feel like if you started with three things and you're ready to add more you have to add three or four more. Just add one more thing if that is all you can do. If you added a couple and you did great with some and fell off with some others, try to add just one of things you fell off doing. Don't overwhelm yourself. Healing is slow and the only way to perform an open heart surgery is to take your time, stay focused, have a good team helping you, and keep going.

Praise For Deliverance

"The Lord is my rock, my fortress, and my deliverer, my God, my rock where I seek refuge, my shield and the horn of my salvation, my stronghold I called to the Lord, who is worthy of praise, and I was saved from my enemies. The ropes of death were wrapped around me; the torrents of destruction terrified me. The ropes of Sheol entangled me; the snares of death confronted me. I called to the Lord in my distress, and I cried to my God for help. From His temple He heard my voice, and my cry to Him reached His ears. Then the earth shook and quaked; the foundations of the mountains trembled; they shook because He burned with anger. Smoke rose from His nostrils, and consuming fire came from His mouth; coals were set ablaze by it. He bent the heavens and came down, total darkness beneath His feet. He rode on a cherub and flew, soaring on the wings of the wind. He made darkness His hiding place, dark storm clouds His canopy around Him. From the radiance of His presence, His clouds swept onward with hail and blazing coals. The Lord thundered from heaven; The Most High made His voice heard. He shot His arrows and scattered them; He hurled lightning bolts and routed them. The

depths of the sea became visible, the foundations of the world were exposed, at Your rebuke, Lord, at the blast of the breath of Your nostrils. He reached down from on high and took hold of me; He pulled me out of deep water. He rescued me from my powerful enemy and from those who hated me, for they were too strong for me. They confronted me in the day of my calamity, but the Lord was my support. He brought me out to a spacious place; He rescued me because He delighted in me. The Lord rewarded me according to my righteousness; He repaid me according to the cleanness of my hands. For I have kept the ways of The Lord and have not turned from my God to wickedness. Indeed, I let all his ordinances guide me and have not disregarded his statutes. I was blameless toward Him and kept myself from my iniquity. So The Lord repaid me according to my righteousness, according to the cleanness of my hands in His sight. With the faithful You prove yourself faithful, with the blameless You prove yourself blameless, with the pure You prove yourself pure, but with the crooked You prove yourself shrewd. For You rescue an oppressed people, but You humble those with haughty eyes. Lord, You light my lamp; my God illuminates my darkness. With You I can attack a barricade, and with my

God I can leap over a wall. God — His way is perfect; the word of the Lord is pure. He is a shield to all who take refuge in Him. For who is God besides the Lord? And who is a rock? Only our God. God — He clothes me with strength and makes my way perfect. He makes my feet like the feet of a deer and sets me securely on the heights. He trains my hands for war; my arms can bend a bow of bronze. You have given me the shield of Your salvation; Your right hand upholds me, and Your humility exalts me. You make a spacious place beneath me for my steps, and my ankles do not give way. I pursue my enemies and overtake them; I do not turn back until they are wiped out. I crush them, and they cannot get up; they fall beneath my feet. You have clothed me with strength for battle; You subdue my adversaries beneath me. You have made my enemies retreat before me; I annihilate those who hate me. They cry for help, but there is no one to save them — they cry to The Lord, but He does not answer them. I pulverize them like dust before the wind; I trample them like mud in the streets. You have freed me from the feuds among the people; You have appointed me the head of nations; a people I had not known serve me. Foreigners submit to me cringing; as soon as they hear they obey me. Foreigners lose heart and come trembling from their fortifications. The Lord lives — blessed be my rock! The God of my salvation is exalted. God — He grants me vengeance and subdues peoples under me. He frees me from my enemies. You exalt me above my adversaries; You rescue me from violent men. Therefore I will give thanks to You among the nations, Lord; I will sing praises about Your name. He gives great victories to His king; He shows loyalty to His anointed, to David and his descendants forever."

(Psalm 18)

6

Setting Boundaries, Not Walls

Every time I had to sit in a courtroom with my ex I felt like I couldn't breathe. I didn't want to look at him and I definitely didn't want him looking at me. Testifying against him for the abuse was done more privately and I still felt scared. Then when he violated the PFA the first time and I had to testify against him in person I was terrified. Especially when the judge decided to let him go for violating the PFA twice in the same day at the courthouse. All I could think was I was stupid for reporting him. Now I've only made him more mad and now I'm more scared.

I completely understood why so many women stay with their abuser for so long at that point. I understood why women would *go back* to their abusive situations. It seems like the one place that could possibly protect you, the judge and j*ustice* system, actually doesn't care about you or your kids at all. Not only did I realize it's *easier* to stay with an abuser, but it *seems* safer! I already had a fear for him while we were married. I was more afraid when he found out I told someone he grabbed my five year old by the throat and threw him and I wanted help escaping. Then even more fear came in when I filed my PFA and they told me he was going to get a copy in the mail with my whole statement! I literally almost ripped up the report and left. And then the state police made a surprise visit to seize all his weapons from the house and again the fear kept getting bigger and bigger it was heard for me to sleep, eat, go anywhere. I was always looking over my shoulder worried about starting my car, worried about being anywhere alone. When he violated the PFA and I was told by the judge himself that they were not going to do anything about it, I felt like a slow gazelle in the middle of an open field surrounded by hungry lionesses just ready to tear me limb to limb.

When the judge evicted him from the house so me and all the kids could have a place to live, I had some men first drive by to make sure he wasn't there for a couple days, then go in the house with me. The feeling of opening the door for the first time was so intense I thought I was going to pass out. I knew they took his guns but I was so scared he got a hold of one and had it rigged to the door or he

somehow knew when I'd be there and just waited until I
came and he'd shoot me.

It didn't happen, thank God, but I had the house checked
for cameras and began to clean and throw out the trash
that was left behind. I barricaded the door for the first
month or so and had an emergent plan to escape should
he break in. He never gave me problems at the house,
thank God, but he did end up seeing us on the highway
and tried to run us off the road. He looked right into my
van and saw me and all the kids, his biological newborn
babies as well, and still tried to run us off the road. Which
was another failed attempt with the justice system. So yes, I
totally understand how abused women *feel* like it would be
safer to stay in abuse than get out. It's easier.

But I didn't want easy. I was stronger than that even
though I didn't feel like I was at the time. I knew I didn't
deserve abuse and more so than me were my kids. They
didn't deserve abuse. God entrusted me to raise them and I
wasn't going to allow them to keep getting abused, grow
bitterness and hatred in their hearts and then grow up to
be an abuser to others. I didn't want my daughters to get
into relationships where they would be abused because
they grew up thinking it was okay since I stayed. God

doesn't want that for His children even more than we don't want it for our children. I watched my mom be abused by her ex husband, not my dad, for more of my life than not. The curse had to stop with me. I had to put my foot down no matter how hard it was and regain my life back, for me, my children, and everyone else who needs help out of the traps too. This was the first setup of my boundaries.

Boundaries are a line that marks the limits of an area. This was my limit. I was done with not being taken seriously and I was done living in fear. I made up my mind that I wasn't going to give up until justice was done. Sure I felt like a fool, I felt anger, I felt unprotected, I felt like giving up, but I chose to fight. Not a fist fight or anything illegal, I just wasn't giving up. I know we did no wrong and I knew God wasn't going to let us down.

God says in His word, *"It is mine to avenge; I will repay. In due time their foot will slip; their day of disaster is near and their doom rushes upon them." "Blessed are those who mourn, for they will be comforted."* Choose to hold on to those promises.

Sometimes making up your mind to set boundaries in place is the hardest part of setting boundaries. But you can do it and you deserve it. You don't have to let the judicial system overlook you as just another docket number, you don't have to give in to your narcissistic mother or mother-in-law, put your foot down with your boss who is making inappropriate remarks to you while holding your job over your head. Tell your doubt and fear that you will not keep quiet, you will not let someone else stay bound to depression and suicide.

You are worth more. Be loud and proud. Stand up for what is right and shut down all that's wrong. You are the answer. You are the cure. You are the one God sent to rescue others. You are the one God put in place to take down the Goliaths in your life and the lives of others. God is taking your weakness and giving you strength. You are the light in the dark places. You are the one others can look up to. You are the lending hand. Even when you can't see it, even when you can't believe it, even when your faith is as small as a mustard seed; or smaller you are God's plan you are God's design. You are the reason that a little girl gets to go home to her family. You are the reason a child no longer has to be scared at night. You are the reason a woman has strength to overcome. And your pain has a purpose. Don't let anyone take that from you. Set boundaries for yourself.

Jesus doesn't tell us *"Heal the sick, raise the dead, cleanse those with leprosy, drive out demons. Freely you received, freely give"* for no reason! He tells us this because in Him we can do all things. He knows what you are capable of. He knows you and wants to use your pain to propel you into your blessing, into your promised land, into your healing and victory.

How do we set boundaries when we've never done it before? I'm considered more introverted and I hate when others are upset with me and I love to help. So setting boundaries for me personally has always been a challenge for as long as I can remember, even when I wasn't intentional about boundaries. This looks like saying "yes," when you really want to say "no," for any number of reasons. Or following with the crowd to keep from being bullied or picked on. Agreeing to things you would never agree to normally but it'll prevent any kind of conflict. Just accepting what's happening to you or around you because *that's just life* or *that's not my business*. Or worse, thinking *oh I'll let them think they won but I know I'm right and he can scream at me and put me down all he wants. He will run out of words soon and shut up*. All of these you should stay far away from ever doing or thinking. It's enabling the abuser and causing nothing but trauma to yourself. Take the first step and *choose* to set boundaries for yourself. Make your mind up that you are going to set a boundary and stick to it no matter what comes against you. You can stay quiet and keep getting hurt or you can stand up for yourself by setting boundaries and become healed. I am going to remind you throughout this book, healing hurts. It all hurts, but healing will become healed and hurt will no longer be there.

I love to travel. Flying has always been one of my favorite ways to escape. That and horseback riding. But every time I fly, before take off the flight attendants remind us in case of emergency we are to put our oxygen mask on before our children. Being a mom, this always gives me chills even though I know and understand the importance of it. I still have such a hard time envisioning myself taking care of myself before my children. But it's the most important way to actually have a chance at saving my children. I completely understand that if I put their oxygen on first and I pass out, I'm of no help and they wouldn't even know what to do. So I get it. Make sure I'm good so I can properly care for them. Yet it's still hard to picture myself physically putting myself first. So of course I always pray I'm never in that situation anyway, because I've had oxygen masks fall while flying before and I can tell you the fear that grips you is indescribable. At least it was for me. Setting boundaries is the same way. You have to take care of yourself first before you'll be any good for your kids, business, ministry and any healthy relationship.

It takes a certain kind of strength to set healthy boundaries and stick to them. Yes, that strong person is you. In your weakness you are made strong. You don't have to feel like it now, but the more you set boundaries the easier it will be and you'll see your true strength.

You will be able to breathe again, feel empowered and confident. Let me tell you, the day I *decided* to be intentional about my boundaries setting, I felt a weight lift off my shoulders by the time I went to bed that evening. The next day I felt like a bird. I thought I already felt free, until I decided to set intentional boundaries.

A quick backstory. I recently hit a burnout season. Thank God it was short, in my opinion, but still long enough. I had wanted to help family and friends and everyone I possibly could because I wanted to feel of use and value. I wanted to make a difference. And there's nothing wrong with that.

Your pain

has a

purpose

However, doing *too* much leads to burnout. So I got myself in a whirlwind of helping so much that I started to become too busy. Busyness turned into my not having time to write this book; then no time to do my hair and get dressed. *Messy messy bun sweats every day.* Then busy became tiring and I'd sleep in past all my morning alarms I enjoyed having set to spend time with God; get myself together, and write this book before the kids woke up. Sleeping-in resulted in not making my bed because I had too much to do and I was always in a rush everywhere. All. Day. Long. My house became messier and during prayer I realized I need my outside life and the inside of me to be organized. I thrive off organization. A family situation came up that was extremely unorganized, to no one's fault. We did the best we could with a last minute life changing situation.

But the fact that there was no organization and everything could change any given minute of the day was stressful for me. I got to a point of losing hope for a day, and for me that's a long time to lose hope since I've started healing. I could see myself going backwards and that was scary for me. Anxiety hit me and I felt like I was just being tossed by the waves and couldn't catch a breath.

I hit a rock bottom moment and reached out to my best friend asking for prayers and help. They invited me over to their house and I packed the kids up faster than I ever have and went to seek help. They prayed for me that night and gave me other resources for different areas I was needing help in. On my drive home I felt so relaxed, so much peace; shalom at its finest and God began to answer my questions. He showed me I was being burned out. I needed to use the word *no* a lot more often and not build walls, but set boundaries. That peace hasn't left me yet. And the first time I got to put my boundary to use and simply say "no" I felt empowered. I felt like I had taken back control. Not from God. Never take control from God.

Take back control of your life. You're not controlling the other person; you're controlling you. And you're not letting anyone or anything get in the way of what God has for you. When my want to help so much turned into a chaotic burnout, it slowed me down to everything else I was supposed to be doing. This book is God's plan and that was the first thing I stepped away from. Getting myself ready in the morning brought me happiness and made me more productive throughout the day. It was one habit I started when I first started my healing process. That too was taken early on. Even spending time with God started to feel rushed. Taking God away is never a good thing. Ever! You see, setting boundaries, like forgiveness, is for you. Of course it has its effects on others as well but we don't set boundaries and we don't forgive, for the other person. Put your oxygen mask and life vest on yourself *first.*

Let your 'yes' mean yes, and your 'no' mean no. You don't have to give a reason. I'm sure you'll want to. But don't fall into that trap either. Giving a lengthy reason often leads to telling a lie. Just simply say "no." If they ask why, simply say "I can't," if you want to show respect or just say "I said no." More than likely you will be asked for a reason. No matter how hard someone pushes you, stand your ground. If anyone can't except your answer, it's not you that has a problem. It's a problem within them, and they clearly don't respect you. A narcissist is a pro at this and will make you feel and think you're the one not being respectful; you're being controlling. They tell you how they would do it for you, it's just this one time, it's not that bad. They *really* need help and you're *the only one* who they trust; the only one they have.

A narcissist will do anything and everything they can to make you fall for their trap again. I speak from experience. If it's over the phone, hang up and block the number if you have to for a while, or silence the notifications from them. Same if it's a text, just silence notifications and don't text back. If it's in person, leave. Get in your car and leave or get an Uber and leave. If they are at your house *tell* them to leave. You can *tell* nicely, but don't make it a question for them to answer with you a "no," and they continue to harass and pressure you.

HEALTHY BOUNDARIES

When God told me to start saying "no" more often I agreed to set boundaries. At first I cut everyone off and God quickly reminded me that that was isolation and not what He meant. So I started brainstorming and asking Him to show me what boundaries really are, and the more specific the better. *Part of my being internally organized.* Boundaries will look different for everyone. But they are all just as highly important.

You may need to stop talking to a particular someone before 8 p.m. every night and not until after 11 a.m. the following day. Or turn your phone notifications off every day at 10 p.m. to sleep well. You may need to delete a social media account or unfollow some people. Block some people. You might have to get out of certain Facebook groups.

You might have to stop hanging out with a friend or family member. Stop going to their house. Stop answering their calls. Or only limit one call a day for three minutes max. You might have to tell someone when to stop gossiping and redirect the conversation or say goodbye and hang up. You might have to stop allowing your kids to visit their toxic parent. Or toxic grandparents. You might have to say "no" to babysitting family and friends' kids for free or all together. Say "no" to having certain people at your house. If they always leave a mess behind, or come over just to lay around and be lazy; or maybe it's someone who gossips or always wants your help but never listens and it becomes draining for you. Say "no" to helping a family member or friend who doesn't help themselves. You know they just want you to do all the work and the more you help the more they ask and then the more things are piled on your plate.

You might have to say "no" to your boss. Stop staying at work longer than what you were hired for. Stop doing tasks that aren't your job description. Of course if this brings you joy, keep at it, but if it's burning you out or irritates you in any way, then say "no." Remember some of these boundaries will look different for everyone. Say "no" to taking your lunch break with that colleague. Tell your boss to stop touching you. You may need to find a new job completely or flat out quit, with or without notice. You might have to stop applying for jobs below your skill level. Believe in yourself. Have confidence in yourself. I dare you to apply to some positions you've always wanted without the experience they are looking for. If it's Gods will He will make them hire you.

You might have to stop eating after 6 p.m. Maybe you need to stop procrastinating. Work out. Go for that daily walk. Read your Bible first thing in the morning and the last thing you do before bed each night. You might have to stop eating out. Stop eating sweets and cut sugars. Every time you're tempted by a brownie, tell it "no." You might have to stop watching tv. Maybe take the whole tv out of your living room or bedroom. Maybe you have to take the tv out of your house completely. Boundaries are for you, remember? So set them for yourself too.

Your boundaries include your children. If they are old enough and capable of doing their own laundry, tell them to do their own laundry from now on. If your boys are peeing all over the seat and floor, show them how to clean it properly and enforce that every time the come out of the bathroom. Obviously that's for older kids too. Your 3-year old may be too young but still old enough to at least try and aim for the inside of the toilet bowl. You may have to say "no" to sleepovers with their friends, or family members. You might have to set a bedtime for your children of all ages. Under 10 years old bedtime is 8 p.m., teens in your room quietly at 9 p.m. and no electronics; and all lights out at 11 p.m. Adult children who live at home, quiet and doors locked at midnight.

These are all examples, you will have to set your own based on your circumstances of course. But doing this is not to control them, it's to give you control of your time. You may want quiet time at 8 p.m. so you can read and take a bath. Lights out at 10 p.m. so you can get actual sleep. Your boundaries might look like no one is allowed out of their room until 8 a.m., so you can get yourself together, pray, maybe check emails before the day starts. You may want to put up a chores chart so everyone can help you out, so you're not so overwhelmed. Plus chores teach kids how to take care of things around the house so when they move out they'll be a whole lot more likely to take care of their own home. Boundaries for your children may even look like homeschooling, or if you already homeschool then maybe a season of public school. Again it's what's best for your own personal circumstances.

Set boundaries now for the future. Future relationships, future friendships, future children if you don't have any yet. You set boundaries now for future careers and business opportunities; future ministries God is preparing you for. By having healthy boundaries now, you will have more success with your future everything. You will not tolerate nearly as many bad, negative and unhealthy relationships. You are preventing being taken advantage of. Red flags will become much easier to notice and run from earlier on. Even in your career choices. You will sit in an interview and know automatically the second they offer you a silver platter with bones and greasy fat on it. Employers will see your confidence and either say "no" to you because they know they won't stand a chance or they will be asking *you* to take the job. That's how you should be treated. If you are a daughter of the Most High, then you are more valuable than any amount of income, any doctoral degree.

Yes, yes, and yes, you can fully believe this about yourself because it's true! And no, no, and no, that doesn't make you conceited just because you believe you are who God says you are! Just be mindful to not be prideful. You don't *have* to negotiate more income because you're a daughter of the King. *Unless they are trying to get over on you.* If your job title and your experience is worth $15 an hour then be blessed and watch what God does in your life anyway. Because He is a good, good Father who loves to give good gifts to those who love and obey Him. The point is to know your true identity and to not be taken advantage of again by setting boundaries.

How do we know what needs a boundary

Just because it's healthy to set boundaries, healthy boundaries, doesn't mean every single thing gets a boundary line per se. Boundaries are best looked at as non negotiables. When God showed me I was burned out and told me I needed to say "no" more often, the first thing I thought was *I'm cutting everyone off, no one is coming in my house and I'm not calling or texting anyone first and I'm saying no to everything.* But that's not healthy. Plus I can negotiate with most things in my life right now. I had to take inventory of *what* and *who* in my life needed boundaries. There are several ways to know.

1. **How does this person or situation make you feel?** When you are around them do they encourage you or put you down? Do their jokes rub you the wrong way? Do they laugh more at you than with you? Do they gossip a lot? Or at all? Do they respect your wishes when it comes to how you want your kids raised or even just simply taking your shoes off in the house? What about situations? Does babysitting stress you out? Are the schools making you wanna pull out your hair? Is homeschool becoming overwhelming? Simply put, do they get on your nerves more than you enjoy being around them? If you answered yes, then your answer is yes. Set a boundary with them.

Also on a side note I homeschool and understand it can be a struggle especially depending what kind of homeschool you choose. If the thought of putting your kids in public school is worse than the daily struggle of homeschool, I recommend you look into unschooling and relaxed homeschooling in your state. Unschooling is legal in the U.S. and it has been the absolute best for me and my children. And they learn so much while I feel no stress at all about it.

2. **Are they supportive?** When you have something to celebrate or a congratulations, do they celebrate and congratulate you? Or do they quickly brush that off to talk about something else? Especially themselves or someone else that they always seem the fondest of. *A sibling or other friend.* Are they quick to always ask you for help but never come to help you when you're in need? If they are focused more on themselves or someone else other than you when you are the topic, you need to set boundaries. If they cry out to you for help all the time but never sacrifice themselves to come help you, they need boundaries. Make "no" your auto response.

3. **Is this person getting you closer to or further away from your goals?** If your goal is to eat healthier, limit how much time and what time of the day you hang out with anyone

who isn't worried about eating healthier. Take note of your self control too. At the beginning of my healthier lifestyle, I had to eat before going to meet with family or friends so I was full and not tempted. As I got a few years under my belt of a strict healthy lifestyle it became much easier for me to be around any food and not be tempted to eat it. This is the beauty of boundaries. They are not permanent brick walls unless they need to be.

When you are starting a new relationship look out for red flags and again know your limits and what's important to you. Is prayer three times a day important to you? Is this new relationship including prayer three times a day, or only one? Or none at all? Are you the one always bringing it up? Or are they initiating it just as much or more? We've talked about the phone but in today's day and age it's a big deal. It's always fun and exciting to get to know someone. Especially someone you like. But again knowing your limits is critical. I can easily talk on the phone all day long, text and video every day with someone I enjoy; but if I don't stop myself I will not be productive in any of the other things that matter to me.

Use your notification silencer anytime you need to get work done, spend time with the kids, study, or get ready for something. (like church, or bed) This will ensure your focus isn't on every text or phone call. The notifications even send automatic messages if you want. You can have it set up to say *I'm away from my phone, I'll get back to you in an hour. Or later. Or as soon as I get done working or driving.* It's my favorite feature. You may have to tell your new love interest no phone calls or texts after 9 p.m. Or whatever time suits your life. Is your family most important? Don't let anyone take you from spending time with your family. Unless your family is unhealthy and unsafe then for your own self, stay away, set boundaries.

Start Setting Boundaries

Take a good inventory of who you need to set a boundary with and how that boundary needs to be set. Start by asking God to show you who and what. Whatever comes to your mind, write it down. Don't dwell on it. Just write it down and move on to step two. You may have already thought of some people or things that need boundaries by the time you got through half of this chapter.

Step 2: Write down what's most important to you in your *personal life* (health, reading, church, skin care, working out, taking walks, travel, finances, photography, hygiene, early morning wake ups, prayer, worshiping, dancing, creating, hobbies, plants, cars, teaching, missions, the list goes on) You will have a lot that are important but think of these more as non negotiable importances.

Step 3: Write down what's most important to you in your *home life* (homeschooling, public schooling, dinners together every night, TVs or none, family game nights, movie nights, being organized, clean or relaxed living, homestead, pets, do you not want alcohol of any kind in the house). This list goes on too. Home life is for anyone even if you don't have kids.

Step 4: Write down what's most important to you about you *family life* (Sunday dinners at moms, birthday parties, game nights, do you want kids, do you have kids, co parenting, family prayer and Bible study, family vacations with your household family and/or extended family, holidays) again the list goes on.

Step 5: Write down what is most important to you in your *career/business life* (working from home, moving up the corporate ladder, owning your own business, travel for work, military, investing, education)

Now that you have one or two, or more, from each step, who in your life is taking you away from those things? Who is talking down about your choice to not go to college? Who is living a life opposite of the life that you value the most? Who is nagging you about not having kids yet? Who is more interested in shopping than saving (if saving is what you value most)? Where are you going that doesn't allow you to grow? Who in your life is uncompromising? Argumentative? Who hates you for getting divorced? Where do you go and feel drained, unwanted, overlooked, unheard, left out?

These are the people, places, and things you need to cut out completely and/or set a boundary with. Remember, setting boundaries is for your protection. It's to help you continue to walk forward, advance, accomplish your goals and God given dreams. Boundaries are designed to *limit* yourself from another person or situation. And always,

always, always set and keep boundaries with all new relationships as well. The sooner you set a boundary the better. With the exercise you just did, it will be much easier to have those boundaries already set in place when entering any new relationship. (Spouse, friend, co workers, boss, in law family)

As you go through life and as you heal, some of your boundaries will change a bit and that's perfectly fine since you are going to change. You are going to grow. You're already getting wiser, stronger, braver, and bolder. You're already healing, overcoming and moving forward. You are a daughter of the Most High. You wear armor as a piece of who you are. Not to be unlovable. Not to be hard hearted. But to be impenetrable. You walk in confidence and glory. You can laugh without fear of the future because you know whose Hand you hold and the Hand that holds you. ADONAI is your source of life and He will never leave or forsake you.

You walk in **confidence** and glory. You can laugh without fear of the future!

7

Step Into Your Purpose

Two years after leaving my ex husband, more than I can count court hearings, appeals, legal fighting, lots of prayer and fasting, studying, healing, setting boundaries, gaining confidence, discovering who I am and who God has called me to be, finding my purpose and calling, and moving forward in life, I slowly stepped into the "dating" scene.

Now I'll be the first to tell you, I am not ready for any serious relationship even now after two years. And I feel better now than I did several years ago when I was at my best, before ever meeting my ex husband.

About 6 years ago I was single, my son was a year old. I got back heavily into fitness and health again after having him; I was thriving, on fire for God and working in ministry that I loved beyond words. Had an amazing group of God fearing women who I called my sisters. It was a high point in my life for sure and I didn't want to lose that. I wanted to stay single and I loved it. I was confident in myself and I knew who I was in Christ. So now at this point in my life, I feel that good again! In many ways a whole lot better. I do miss having more time to hang out with friends but everyone has kids and now all my friends are married, so it makes it a bit harder to really hang out.

A quick example is Valentine's Day, which I absolutely LOVE! But now I need some single friends so we can celebrate together without taking away Valentine's Day from the married folks. Lol. But that's how I got into this "dating" world.

I'm going to tell you a bit of what this looks like and why it's important to step into. Believe it or not, it's been helping with my healing process! I use the word "dating" because ultimately dating is supposed to be spending regular time with someone you're interested in or have romantic feelings for. But if you join today's dating world (2023), dating is getting to know someone; finding someone you have similar interests in. Opening yourself up to allow someone else into your life with the *intention* of keeping them there long term. And it takes a lot of time. For the majority of people. Dating is not an easy thing to step into and it can be very discouraging if you are looking for that romantic partner or, like I am, friendships and connections.

I almost named this chapter "Don't Skip This Chapter" but then I didn't want everyone to jump here and start reading it first. As a Christian in my first church, I was always told dating is this bad thing. I understood why they thought that way about dating because it can be very ugly and lead to lots of sin quickly if you use it in the wrong way. Just like how you can use technology or social media. Some people have success on social media and use it for good while others use it for *evil*. I'll just leave that there. You get the point.

Dating in my experience can be used either way as well. Also keep in mind how I described dating. I am not in a church where the opportunity to meet new friends is really available. I work from home and homeschool and it can get pretty lonely at times. But I'm ready to "date" now. I'm ready to let others in. I'm ready to get to know other people and make friends and share common interests. I'm ready to be around others who I can share life with, whether for a season, or a lifetime. I'm ready to get a babysitter and go have a girls' brunch or meet for dinner.

Dating now is more than just finding a boyfriend or girlfriend, going out to dinner and movies, and hooking up or moving on with no intention of marriage. Dating is now lunches together on Zoom, group hangouts at the bowling alley with men and women, getting together with the girls and going to get coffee while working on our businesses together. It's meeting up at the park with your kids, picnics with homeschool families. Dating has now become finding boy *friends* and girl *friends.* If you are using dating for good.

I joined a singles Christian group and it's been so fun. You can engage in others' concerns, laugh at funny "romantic dating" fails; celebrate in their romantic successes, encourage one another, make other female friends, and so much more! My favorite thing is that I can talk with men *and* other women without feeling like it's something romantic or leading that way. It's so nice that other women want to make single female friends as well. And if you *want* to start pursuing someone with a romantic interest then try it out. But this has given me the opportunity to test boundaries and be open and honest and overcome some fears. (Like telling people I'm divorced and have four kids) That used to be something I'd rather not offer up unless asked, in fear of being judged by other Christians especially. Yes it's a thing and yes it's happened to me already. Now I'm putting myself out there and finding other divorced single moms and making friendships, some just over the phone and some close by in my area which is another great way to use social media and technology for good. FaceTime movie nights, FaceTime Bible studies, FaceTime prayers and conversations are just as meaningful as in person.

When the time is right and you feel you're ready to push yourself a bit more out of your comfort zone and start letting people *in,* then "dating" as I explained it can be very beneficial for you. And if you try it out and then realize *it's too soon I'm not ready after all.* Then stop, get out the group, delete the app, and you can always try again later. But when you are ready, just take baby steps. And I use "dating" as an example because that's a hot topic and what's currently working for me moving forward in life; and I'm enjoying it. It's what I struggled with and feared I'd never make girl friends and I can never talk to men or if I did it had to be a very small "hi" and "have a good day" type of conversation. *Or lack of conversation I should really say.* But God calls us to community. So this is me stepping out into community and putting a nail in the head of the enemy that put those ridiculous fears in my head! It may look completely different for everyone depending on what that thing looks like for you to step into, and the season you're in.

Maybe it's time to jazz up your resume and start applying for positions you deserve, but don't think you'll get. Start walking into places and personally hand the boss or even owner of the company your resume. It may be time for you to start your ministry at your church or out of your own home. Start that small group or prayer group. Go out and start asking people you see in the store if you can pray for them. Maybe it's time you reach out to strangers and start getting resources together to start your nonprofit. Maybe it's time you quit your job and jump into your own business. Or quit your job, sell your things and travel. It may be time for you to buy a nice ring light and start doing your makeup on camera or start your YouTube page, write your book, apply to be a foster parent or look into adoption, buy the storefront, buy the camper, start your Airbnb. Whatever it is that makes you wonder if it's even possible for someone like *you*. Just take that one step *into* it.

The enemy has held you back far too long. He's kept your heart, mind and body in chains. It's time to break free and step into your anointing. Step into your calling, your purpose, step into your promised land! You called upon the

Lord. He heard your cries. He reached down and rescued you. Now walk away from that mess He rescued you from. He has prepared a place for you that overflows with milk and honey. It's *yours!* He prepared a table for you! And not just any table. This ***table*** is a peace treaty that separates you from this cursed earth in the presence of your enemies; to show them He loves you and fulfills His promise. The Lord says, "I have called you by name, YOU ARE MINE."

You don't belong to the things of this world. Or the lies of the enemy. Praise God He *wants* nothing but good for you. He is handing you a free gift that you don't deserve (none of us do), but He does it anyway because He delights in you. You are His daughter, a royal priesthood, a holy nation, a light to this dark world. Now step into what He gave you. Accept His gifts. He not only gives you these beautiful blessings but He prepares you as well. He clothes you with strength and makes your way perfect. You may not see it now but when it comes to a finish you will see. So bring it to a finish. Close that door and use your experience with abuse and your experience with God's great goodness to help others. He sets your feet *securely* on the heights and *trains* your hands for war. Your arms can bend a bow of bronze. Meaning whatever hardships come your way,

It's time to break *free* and step into your *anointing*

He has prepared you to defeat and overcome them. Abuse, you break it. Cancer, you break it. PTSD, you break it. Suicide, you break it. He clothes you with strength for battles. These things fall beneath you and can't get up. They literally don't stand a chance. The Lord gives victory to His anointed. To you child of God. Take pride in the Lord and stand firm. The Lord is your shepherd and you have all you need. He lets you lie down in green pastures. He leads you beside quiet waters and renews your life. He leads you along the right paths for His namesake. Even when you go through the darkest valley, you will fear no evil, because God is with you, His rod and His staff, comfort you, He anoints your head with oil and your cup overflows; only goodness in faithful love will pursue you all the days of your life, and you will dwell in the house of The Lord as long as you live; should you choose Him.

You know your true identity, you forgave others and you forgave yourself; you set up the boundaries; now it's time to shine. It's time to trust again. The Lord is telling you that you can trust Him. You don't have to trust anyone else. But you *can* trust Him. He has proven Himself trustworthy, honest, upright, just and time and time again that He fulfills His promises. He wants you to trust His people also because they are a reflection of Him. But even if you don't trust a single soul on the earth right now, He just wants you to trust Him. Take His hand. It's before you reaching out, just waiting for you to grab hold so He can lead you exactly to the place He has prepared for you. The Lord says *I have called you for a righteous purpose, and I will hold you by your hand. I will watch over you and I will anoint you to be a covenant for the people in a light to the nations in order to open blind eyes, and bring out prisoners from the dungeons, and those sitting in darkness from the prison house. I am the Lord. You are precious in My sight and honored and I love you. I am the first and I am the last there's no God but Me.* You can trust Him.

Stepping into

This will be one of the last times you grab your journal for this book. But it won't be the last time you open it, read it, add to it, or apply it to your life. Today I want you to step out in faith. If you made it this far I know your healing has begun even if it's just the seed that was planted by your taking in the promises of God up to this point. Healing has begun.

What is holding you back from taking the next step, or the first step, into the desires of your heart? Your calling? Your purpose?

Whatever answer you gave, does that line up with your true identity? I guarantee not. Or else you wouldn't be limiting yourself. Maybe you just flat out don't want to, but you feel like it's something you're supposed to do or God straight told you to. Like for me it was writing this book. I was told I should write a book back in my early twenties. All the way up until I felt God leading me to writing a book and then getting confirmation several times. I didn't want to write a book so much so that when I finally gave in, I asked God for several more confirmations. It only took that one confirmation and He knocked some sense into me. God is so faithful that after the one confirmation that made me say okay yeah I'm writing a book for sure; He still sent several more confirmations anyway. He knows me.

I know there's someone reading this with terminal cancer and other deadly diseases trying to figure out where you stand. Wanting and hoping for something so much more but you feel that you have nothing to give. Remember you are not *helpless*! You still have your ideas. Your thoughts and desires too. You can still pursue your passions. It may not look the way you envision it. And it may not pan out the way you desire it to be yet or ever. But there are ways you can still reach the world. Paul spent a lot of time in prison and he wrote a good portion of the New Testament in the Bible. And there are many others who have done exceptional things in their limitations. Maybe it's time *you* write your book. Ask every nurse and doctor that comes into your room if you can pray for them. Where do you see a need? See who you can talk to and help fulfill that need. Make a book of poems that will help others who are battling to survive.

I pray God opens your eyes and heart to hear what He would love for you to do. I pray in Jesus' name He would heal every sickness, disease, tissue, blood cell, ligament, organ, bone, and marrow in you right now; and that your faith would be increased so that you and everyone around you would know that He is The Lord your God.

Write down what you're going to do next. Jazz up your resume and apply for your dream position. Call the school you want to attend and schedule a meeting with them. Write your resignation letter. Go look at RV's and have a moving sale. Take the courses to get that certification you've been wanting. Start your business. Sell your artwork. Start your artwork. Move. Book the plane ticket. Start your nonprofit. Pray for the next person you see. And the person after. Write your online course material. Start your YouTube channel. Call the adoption agency. Start the foster care process. Buy a chicken. Start your homestead. Donate to a cause that moves your heart. *Some of my favorites are Destiny's Rescue and Our Rescue, both for sex trafficking.*

How do I know my calling and purpose

So maybe I should have done this first but it's still important that I add it into this chapter. I didn't realize what my purpose and calling was for 31 or 32 years of my life. I'm not much older now so really all my life basically. I knew all the things I loved and the things I couldn't stand. I grew up wanting to be a vet, a model and a pilot. As I got older and realized there were so many other professions in the world, I became lost in a sea of ideas that I would absolutely love. And if you're like that also then you know how tough that really is. It almost makes you waste time because you try to figure out where you belong for so long. Or you don't succeed at much because you try everything and are so anxious to try something else. But when we focus on our actual calling and purpose, we have much more success in life.

Success means accomplishing what you set out to do.

If you want to wake up at 4 a.m. to work out every day, but you wake up at 6 a.m. most days; however you still get a workout in on those days, you succeeded. If you want to read 10 pages in a book every night but some nights you can only read 2 pages, that's still a success. What would be a "fail" is not reading your book at all, not working out at all, not pursuing your dreams at all. I want to help you find your calling and purpose the way that helped me the most. Once you get this, decision making will become easier. And you can take the right steps forward in the direction you should go.

Ask yourself these questions.

1. What do you love so much, you would do for free?
    Even if you don't have the means now, think outside
    the box. The bigger picture. What *would* you do for
    free?

2. What do you see that needs to change or be
    corrected? What we often hate reveals what we are
    called to correct. The things we can't tolerate are
    the things we are called to change.

3. What breaks your heart? We are called to heal the
    things that make us cry. These are the things that
    break our heart so much that we have to know
    more about it.

This may take you a while to really think about, so I
encourage you to take your time. You may know right away
what these answers are and that's great! You may have
never thought about yourself and now you really need to

find *you*. And that's great! Either way, just don't skip this step.

Here is mine that I did a while ago and it makes perfect sense for me.

1. If I could do anything for free, I would travel the world, take photos, tell about God's goodness and help everyone I could!
2. When people don't understand who they are created to be, misusing the Word, women get abused and mistreated, and not knowing their true identity, are all things I feel need to be changed and however I can help bring this change, I will!
3. Sex trafficking and abused women and children break my heart.

Once you have your list, you can now put it into a phrase. Here is mine.

My purpose and calling is to spread the Word of God to women and children who have been and are being abused and mistreated so they know their true identity and heal.

Once I did this all the dots connected and I immediately saw how God was turning all the bad in my life into something good. Bringing light into darkness. Turning what was meant for evil into something good. Graves to gardens. Beauty from ashes. Making His glory known. Using my pain to heal the broken.

Your purpose and calling is just as important and significant. I'm so excited for you!

8

I Am Free

Although I'd never want to go through all that I've been through ever again; I will say that I'm so blessed to be able to help others who are suffering. I can relate to you. I feel your suffering. I have asked the same questions you ask. I know the torture. I've been there screaming and crying in my bed tossing and turning asking God to take this pain or take me, just kill me I can't take it anymore. I know the drowning feeling. I know the claustrophobic feeling when you're in a wide open space. I know the feeling of being so far gone as if you're lost in outer space in a room full of people. I know the suicidal thoughts. I felt all your pain. I also know there is light at the end of this tunnel. I know there's brighter days. I know joy. I am filled with joy and hope. I know what it's like to dance in the storm. I feel the chains break free. I feel the love. I know peace. No matter where you are in your journey, just know these are yours as well.

The Oxford Languages defined the word freedom as, *the power or right to act, speak, or think as one wants* **without hindrance or restraint**. *The state of not being imprisoned or enslaved.* Abuse has no hold on us, fear has no hold on us. We are no longer imprisoned or enslaved to the enemy and his puppets who try to bring us down. You can walk in beautiful freedom!

You are not things that have happened to you. You are chosen and loved. You are heard and cared for. I've personally prayed for you the whole time writing this book and I continue to keep you in my prayers. If I could physically hug you, I would wrap my arms around you and hold you tight.

You are free. You don't deserve to ever

go back. You never deserved those horrible things that happened to you. Whether you're out of abuse, and you're starting your healing journey; you're in the middle of your healing journey, you're completely healed and moved on, or if you're still in it debating if you should leave, how you should leave and when you should leave. You may be wondering if it's even possible for *you*, just know that you are worth more and you'll always be worth more than abuse. You don't need that abuser. You don't need those friends. You don't need the family members. You don't need your abusive older children. You don't need that job. This one is for someone very specific, so don't all lash out, but you need to hear this; you don't need that specific church. You don't need the drugs, you don't need the alcohol; you don't need cigarettes, you don't need the sex, you don't need the porn. Again, this one is for someone very specific. This is your confirmation; you do not need that money.

All you need is love. And although you think those things make you feel loved or those people tell you that they love you, and in some ways, they may even "show you." But that's not real love. Love is patient, love is kind. It does not envy, it does not boast, and it is not proud. Love does not dishonor others, it is not self-seeking; it is not easily angered, and it keeps no record of wrongs. Love is not abusive. Love is not condemning. There is no fear in love. There is no torment in love. There is no trauma in love.

You've made it this far through the book, which means you were already on your healing journey, if you hadn't started before. Go back and apply all these tools and resources, and intentionally heal for yourself, for your children, for your future, for your life. And don't go back. And I don't just mean back to the same person, place, or people; I mean don't go back to abuse.

This happens to so many of us so often because we don't fully heal and we look for another person or another thing to fill the void and cover up the pain. But healing is not treated with a bandage. Like I said before healing hurts. It takes time. You have to dig in deep to uproot the infection, the abuse, the trauma, the memories, the hurting the pain, the suffering, and suicide. Allow yourself, (heart, body, mind and soul) to heal properly so you don't replace one abuser for another.

Pay attention to triggers. This is a daily lifelong practice. If you can intentionally identify triggers, you can overcome and heal much faster. We spoke earlier on how to be mindful of what you watch on tv, what you hear on the radio or someone else's conversation that you overhear in a store. It might be an ad that you see or a social media video or post.

I remember driving somewhere and a commercial came on the radio that was advertising a cookout, and it made me instantly feel sad. Normally cookouts are a fun gathering with friends and family. So to combat this sad feeling, I had to play that commercial back in my head and dissect what they were talking about. It didn't take me very long before I realized that the last church cookout event was at an old church that I went to and loved dearly at the time; but the sad part came in because that particular church had deeply hurt me when God was telling us it was time to leave there. My body and my memory had a joyful experience at this church cookout; however, because of the church hurting me that commercial triggered that hurt. Although I had gone through many practices of forgiving them and praying for true forgiveness towards them, something was still not fully healed from that.

So I acknowledged it. I asked God to help me to forgive. I went through a list of forgiving people from that church. Even the ones that didn't do anything to necessarily hurt me, but I wanted to cover all ends as much as possible because I want to heal. Then I began asking God to show me where that hurt was coming from. I do believe that I forgave them but because that wound was a newer healing wound, it was still tender. If you've ever had surgery or stitches, you know that after the skin has healed, the stitches dissolved, or been taken out, the scar doesn't hurt, but it still has a numbing sort of weird sensation. There still a tenderness. But it's closed, there's nothing that can get in. I can't get infected again, and nothing needs to be taken out, so it is healed; it's just not quite 100% *yet*. And this is how our own healing process is also. So be very mindful of the things that trigger you so that you can continue to go through all of the steps on healing and recognize which ones are completely healed. Which ones are tender, which ones need a little bit of attention, and which ones need a whole lot of attention.

I just have to say that I am so proud of you for taking the step into healing. I'm so proud of you for trying. I'm so proud of you for not giving up. I'm proud of you for wanting to want to know more. Every single little step that you take all adds up and it all matters and it all counts. You are so brave. You are so courageous. You are fearfully and wonderfully made. You are beautiful and strong and smart and intelligent. You are an overcomer. You are a hard worker. As long as you have breath in your lungs, it's never too late. I'm so excited for what God has planned for you.

The enemy hits you because he knows who you are. The enemy tries to pull you down because even he knows and believes the word of God is true in the calling, purpose and promises that God has on your life. When your feet hit the ground every morning, the enemy trembles. The enemy lurks and waits for you trying to plan attacks to mess up the plans that God has for you. And to get you further from God and further from your calling. But you have the authority to crush the serpent's head. You have the authority to stand firm on the word of God and declare and decree that the enemy must flee in Jesus' name. You are a warrior. You are victorious. You have already survived the worst days of your life. You are overcoming and you are healing. You can move mountains. You can slay Giants. You are armed and ready for battle. You just have to show up. The Lord is the one who fights for you. You just have to show up and trust in Him.

I want you to say these last three words as every woman across the world reads this and is on one accord declaring and believing in Jesus' name with you right now at this very moment. And don't just whisper these words. Don't just say these quietly to yourself. Say these last three words like you mean it. Like you believe it. Because they are true. These last three words are who I am. Who she is. Who they are. Who *you* are. Say these last three words with the *authority* that you *have*. You say these last three words as justice for your abusers, as justice for your trauma. Say these last three words as a declaration. And not just say them, but *shout* these last three words as a promise. Shout these last three words with me, and all the women across the world in one accord to shake the heavens and earth, to rattle the cages of darkness, to break every chain, to let the glory of God fall on us bringing heaven to earth! Get ready to shake the ground! Get ready to make the devil mad! Get ready for your breakthrough!

1...

2...

3....

I

AM

FREE

You are so courageous. You are fearfully and wonderfully made. You are beautiful and strong and smart and intelligent. You are an

overcomer

God bless you and keep you. May His face shine upon you and give you peace. May He guide you all the days of your life as you commit yourself to Him and His goodness. I pray you see yourself through His eyes and forgive and love with the heart of Christ. I pray supernatural blessings on your soul, mind and body in Jesus' name that He would bring healing to your heart, mind, and physical healing to your body, organs, cells and tissue in Jesus' name. I pray you would see His hand, work and favor in your life like never before, from this day forward and He would remind you of all His glory and protection from days prior, so that He would be glorified. I pray for peace, health and healing in your home, finances, career and relationships. I pray He would open doors for you that no man can shut and close off all things that aren't for you and the plans He has for you. I rebuke all distractions and noise getting in the way of the Lord's voice and your ears, mind and heart so that you would hear what He is telling you and where He is guiding you clearly, in Jesus' name!

Blessed are the poor in spirit, for theirs is the kingdom of heaven.

Blessed are those who mourn, for they will be comforted.

Blessed are the meek, for they will inherit the earth.

Blessed are those who hunger and thirst for righteousness, for they will be filled.

Blessed are the merciful, for they will be shown mercy.

Blessed are the pure in heart, for they will see God.

Blessed are the peacemakers, for they will be called children of God.

Blessed are those who are persecuted because of righteousness, for theirs is the kingdom of heaven.

"Blessed are *you* when people insult you, persecute you and falsely say all kinds of evil against you because of Me. Rejoice and be glad, because great is your reward in heaven." (Matthew 5:3-12)

STAY CONNECTED

Just because this book is at the end, doesn't mean your healing is finished. Stay connected! You can find me on most social media platforms by going to https://msha.ke/bguary

I'd love to hear from you! You can share your testimonies by sending them to my email

at, **BreakingFree.Testimonies@gmail.com**

IDENTITY AND CORRESPONDING VERSES

John 1:12-13; Colossians 3:12; Romans 8:17; 1 Peter 2:9; Isaiah 43:1; John 15:16; Phillipians 3:20; Ephisians 1:3; Ephisians 3:12; Romans 5:1; Phillipians 4:19; Ephisians 1:11; 2 Corinthians 1:21-22; Psalm 23:1-6; Romans 8:37; 2 Timothy 1:7; Ephisians 1:5-8; Isaiah 43:2 ; Isaiah 43:4; Mark 11:24; Psalms 1:3; Matthew 10:8;

If you are a child of God, then you're heirs—heirs of God and fellow heirs with Christ. You are God's chosen one, holy and beloved, with a compassionate heart, kindness, humility, meekness, and patience. You are a chosen race, a royal priesthood, a holy nation, a people for his possession, so that you may proclaim the praises of The One who called you out of darkness into His marvelous light. The Lord who created you and formed you says, "Fear not for I have redeemed you; I have called you by name, you are Mine" He chose you and appointed you so that you should go and bear fruit. And whatever you ask the Father in Jesus name, He may give it to you. Your citizenship is in heaven. He has blessed you in Christ with every spiritual blessing in the heavenly places. You have boldness and access with confidence through your faith in Him. Since you have been justified by faith, you have peace with God through Jesus Christ. God will supply every need of yours according to His riches in glory in Christ Jesus. You have obtained an inheritance. You were predestined according to the purpose of Him who works all things according to the counsel of His will. It is God who establishes you in Christ, and He has anointed you, and has also put His seal on you and given you His Spirit in your heart as a guarantee. The Lord is your shepherd. He makes you lie down in green pastures. He leads you beside still waters. He restores your soul. He leads you in paths of righteousness for His name's sake. Even though you walk through the valley of the shadow of death, you will fear no evil, because God is with you; His rod and His staff, *comfort* you. God prepares a table before you in the presence of your enemies; and He anoints your head with oil. Your cup overflows because He gives you so much. You are more than a conqueror. God gave you a spirit of power and love and self-control; not fear. He predestined you for adoption to Himself as a daughter through His glorious grace, with which He has blessed you in the Beloved. In Him you have redemption through His blood, the forgiveness of your trespasses, according to the riches of His grace, which He lavished upon you, in all wisdom and insight. "When you pass through the waters, I will be with you, and the rivers will not overwhelm you. When you walk through the fire, you will not be scorched, and the flame will not burn you." Says The Lord. "Because you are precious in my sight and honored, and I love you," says The Lord. "Therefore I (Jesus) tell you, everything that you pray and ask for — believe that you have received it and it will be yours." You are like a tree planted beside flowing streams that bears its fruit in its season, and its leaf does not wither. Whatever you do prospers.